Dog to Dog
Communication

The Right Way to Socialize Your Dog

Jamie Shaw

Founder of The Dog School

THE LYONS PRESS
Guilford, Connecticut
An imprint of The Globe Pequot Press

The Lyons Press is an imprint of The Globe Pequot Press.

10 9 8 7 6 5 4 3 2 1

Printed in the United States of America

Designed by Mimi LaPoint

ISBN: 978-1-59921-088-9

Library of Congress Cataloging-in-Publication Data is available on file.

Dog to Dog
Communication

For Brody Bear

and Amazing Grace

Amazing Grace (left) and Brody Bear (right)
Credit: *Finest Image, Essex, VT*

Beloved companions: Kismet and Grace,
two dogs completely at peace with each other.
Credit: Sarah D. Todd

Contents

Foreword

This morning two large, unknown dogs loped into my yard—a Labrador Retriever and a Golden Retriever. Two of my dogs immediately attacked them, and the intruders instinctively fought back. It looked and sounded very dangerous—a rough and tumbling pile of four big dogs, snarling and growling loudly. The altercation seemed to last forever, probably five full seconds, and then it was over. The dogs separated into their original pairings—intruders and home dogs—and the intruders trotted away. Amazingly, not a single drop of blood was shed.

The dogs didn't even have any evidence of saliva on their coats. Was this interaction normal? Was this dog behavior okay? *Yes!* These dogs were simply communicating; they weren't engaging in warfare. Each one of them had exquisite control of his or her teeth. In all that adrenaline-fueled chaotic movement, no tooth actually met flesh. Instead, the home dogs told the intruders to leave at once. The intruders said they didn't like being bossed around and didn't want to leave. A shuffle ensued and the dogs had it out with each other until the unwanted visitors decided they had endured enough. I suspect all four dogs actually enjoyed the encounter.

As dog care providers, we all need to know, understand, and *accept* this normal dog behavior. There is nothing the matter with it. It's not dangerous. It's not even rude. It's simply dogs communicating in the very effective way that they do (and always have done).

Until I took Jamie Shaw's course called "Dog to Dog Communication," I didn't recognize that most of the posturing dogs do is usually just, according to Jamie, "sound and fury signifying nothing." I have now taken Jamie's class with two different dogs and have helped teach the program five or six times. It is absolutely fascinating to see the many and varied ways in which dogs communicate, fuss with each other, and work out their differences without inflicting injury.

A lot of first-time dog owners buy a puppy and then hope for the best. I choose to adopt adult dogs instead. Before I make a lifetime commitment to a dog, I want to *know* the dog's adult temperament and personality. That makes it possible to select nonaggressive dogs with a fair amount of certainty, particularly when

Jamie will evaluate them for me. (Of course, I have fallen in love with a few dog-aggressive dogs and adopted them anyway!)

With a puppy, you usually can't be as certain. Breed doesn't always tell you very much. To the best of my knowledge, despite all the work on the canine genome, no geneticists have proved that there is any genetic predisposition to aggression. The statistics of Kelley Bollen, owner and director of Animal Alliances, LLC, bear this out—there is only a very slight difference in the likelihood of aggressive behavior between the most aggressive and least aggressive breeds in her study. (In a small sample of various breeds, roughly 80 percent of the bully breeds were non-aggressive, compared to 90 percent of the retrievers.)

With that said, this is why Jamie's book is so important for all dog care providers. Regardless of breed, she encourages us to socialize our dogs as much and as early as possible. She shows us ways to train our dogs to behave appropriately in situations where multiple dogs are present. She effectively teaches us how to properly manage our dog-aggressive dogs and, most importantly, she opens our eyes to the fact that dogs should be allowed to communicate with each other—it's in their nature.

Our world would be much better for dogs if humans were more open to letting them communicate with one another. Like people, most dogs can have their disagreements and tiffs without hurting each other. It's my fervent hope that *Dog to Dog Communication* will enable more people to understand dog to dog communication as thoroughly as Jamie does. We—and our dogs—will all have richer, fuller lives when we learn to really understand dog to dog communication for what it is.

Lisa Barrett,
Top Dog Agility Instructor

Acknowledgments

To my husband, Drew Bloom, and my daughter, Halle Bloom. Thank you for your daily encouragement, laughter, light, and energy; helping me to find the time to write; always being there; and most of all for loving me so endlessly.

For their unconditional love and for teaching me to believe I could do anything and get anywhere: my parents, Sheila Brand and Leonard Shaw.

For amazing friendship, daily support, and encouragement: Sam Punchar, Lisa Barrett, and Claudia Hundsdoerfer-Abae.

For the dogs with whom I've had the blessing of sharing my life: Koko, Mickey, Brody, Grace, Kismet, Yoda, Dutch, Mimi, Tara, Tucker, Wyatt, Kobe, Oscar, Pippit, and Jigs.

For spiritual and emotional support and for love: John Hopkins.

For answering my endless questions, giving great editorial support, and believing I could write this book when I wasn't so sure: Kaleena Cote.

For being in my life and being part of who I am today: Art Shaw, Gary Shaw, the late Bob Shaw, Irwin Noparstak, Raymond Brand, Sandra Pitman, Charles and Sharon Bloom, Anne Bueche, Shara Tarule, Amy Branch, Renee Reiner, Laura Lomas, and Nancy Hammond.

For teaching me most of what I know about dog to dog behavior although she'll never take credit for it: Margaret Libby.

For their friendship and for their land to run on without which I'd be insane: Liz and Deb Wilding.

For all the people too numerous to name that are quoted in my book: thank you.

For phenomenal photos: Demmie Todd and Detlev Hundsdoerfer.

For all the dogs and their companions who have taught me and touched my life and my heart I am grateful.

Yoda, the Bulldog, gives his most endearing look as Penny, the hound, curiously watches him.
Credit: Sarah D. Todd

Introduction

But he was wagging his tail. It wasn't until a few years later that I learned to ask, "*How* was he wagging his tail?" Brody Bear always wagged his tail when he was about to fight with another dog. I owe so much of what I now know about dog to dog communication from living with Brody Bear.

I got Brody when I worked at a kennel that was also the pound for the county I lived in. He was a stray that had been picked up by animal control. I fell in love with him the moment I saw him, and as time passed and no one ever claimed him, I decided to take him home with me. Brody began going to work with me every day. He was constantly playing and really seemed to enjoy being in the company of other dogs. But then, out of nowhere, when he was about two years old, he became dog-aggressive.

It started with small altercations—little spats with other dogs—but then it progressed to full blown fights. I used to go hiking with Brody, off leash, every day in a local park or on the Long Trail or at a beach. It didn't matter where we went—I just found a way to have him off leash and getting exercise everyday. When

he started fighting, I still took him off his leash. It was only an occasional thing, and while I was upset, I couldn't imagine a life with my dog being leashed all the time. Off-leash exercise felt like a required part of our existence. But Brody's fighting got worse. And worse. I started to fear going anywhere with him. He hadn't injured another dog, but I realized that was only a matter of time. So I started keeping Brody leashed while on our walks in the woods. Sadly, this once fun activity became a chore instead of a pleasure.

Brody continued to try to fight with other dogs, but being on his leash, he couldn't. It was still no fun walking him. His obedience was pretty good—he knew how to walk on a leash without pulling, and he knew the basic commands for sit, down, and stay, but he sure didn't know how to act around other dogs. Feeling frustrated and scared, I turned to a local obedience instructor for help.

I signed up for class wondering how I was ever going to make it in a room full of dogs. The first week there were no dogs present, and I was shocked to see about forty people at the class. I feared the second week, but choke chain in hand, I showed up with Brody. As soon as Brody saw the other dogs, he went crazy—lunging and barking and pulling like mad. The instructor immediately came over to me and told me to throw Brody to the ground and pin his neck down with my knee.

Now, I knew how to obedience train a dog; I had been doing it since I was seven years old. But I had never dealt with an aggressive dog before. I did as the instructor said and pinned Brody to the ground, hating it as I did so, but doing it just the same. And so class went. I pinned Brody every time he went after another dog. I continued to go to class, and Brody's lunging improved a slight bit. I practiced his obedience all the time, and that improved immensely. But out of class, in the real world, Brody got no better. I would pin him down when he showed aggression toward other dogs in parks or on trails, but he seemed to be getting worse. He could heel and sit and stay and come from a stay, but he couldn't walk down the sidewalk without causing us both a ton of grief.

I went to another trainer who said to do the same thing. This trainer had me work on a long rope to practice our obedience safely, and she had me continue to pin Brody down. I continued his obedience training and even got to the point where Brody could stay in a line-up of dogs with me out of sight (this is an exercise done in formal obedience competitions). Brody wouldn't move, and I could trust him to hold that stay no matter what. But I still couldn't walk down the street with him.

I spoke with more trainers. No one seemed to have any suggestions, except that my first trainer wanted me to use a shock collar on Brody. I couldn't *imagine* shocking my best friend.

Over the years that I was doing all this training with Brody, I began to offer private obedience lessons at the kennel where I was working. There was no Internet then, but I started attending dog seminars and trying to learn everything I could about dogs and dog behavior. The problem was that no one seemed to have any new ideas on how to deal with dog aggression.

I loved my boy more than anything in the world and wanted to fix his problem. Pinning him only made him more submissive to me. It never stopped his aggression. I felt frustrated, scared, and, well, *embarrassed* to walk him anywhere. I could take him to the dog training club to which I belonged and he was fine, but I couldn't take him anywhere else.

I continued to do private training with some people who boarded their dogs at the kennel, and it was going so well that I decided to offer a few outdoor classes at the kennel in the owner's big yard. Classes were such a success that I found a town hall where I could have indoor classes, and moved into that space when the weather got cold.

And so began The Dog School. It was called Canine K–12 back then. I changed the name in 2003 because no one could remember Canine K–12. What I wanted more than anything was to offer a kinder, more loving method for training dogs. I wanted to stop pinning my dog and stop using a choke chain and find a better, gentler way of getting cooperation from my best friend. And more than anything I *really* wanted Brody's aggression to stop.

It was a few years after The Dog School started that dog trainers in the United States began using food to train their dogs. And we learned to rely on the scientific methods of B. F. Skinner and his discoveries on operant conditioning. His studies showed us that any animal could best be trained by slowly shaping new behaviors. And the best way to do this was to use food and toys to train dogs. Before about 1990, almost no one in the United States used food to train his or her dogs. We all used choke chains and a lot of pushing and pulling. And we used that pinning technique, which made our dogs timid with us but not better with other dogs. That technique, "alpha rolling," is still used by some people today, but it's considered by good, modern trainers to be an outdated, unnecessary way to influence our dogs. Trust me: it sure didn't make Brody better with other dogs.

I learned that I had to "read" my dog. I had to learn to understand his signals and signs, and how he was feeling when he saw another dog. I didn't need to throw him to the ground every time he saw another dog. I learned to understand how he was feeling by understanding what his body was saying. I learned to "speak dog."

The Dog School now offers several different types of classes. We offer regular obedience training and agility classes. But we also offer two levels of classes for dogs who have issues with other dogs. One class is called the Spirited Dog class. It's designed for dogs who are often good with other dogs but have issues upon greeting or at some point in their play. The other class is called the Dog to Dog Communication class (DDC). It used to be called Conquering Dog to Dog Aggression, but dog to dog aggression can't always be conquered—it can be *managed*, but not always conquered.

The DDC class is for dogs that are moderately to seriously aggressive with other dogs. Some of the dogs in that class have injured other dogs; some have just displayed behaviors that made it appear likely that they would hurt other dogs. In both the Spirited Dog class and the DDC class, owners learn all about dog behavior, causes of aggression, types of aggression, and how to try to rehabilitate their dogs to be better with other dogs. They also learn how to manage their dogs' behavior, especially if they have realized that their dogs will never be good with other canines.

At The Dog School we also offer private, one on one behavioral consultations. Sometimes there is not a class soon enough to help someone. Other times, people just want to meet alone. It's very upsetting to have a dog that has issues. People are embarrassed and afraid if their dogs do not relate well to others. While we specialize in helping aggressive dogs (toward other dogs or people) we also work with non-aggressive dogs in both classes and behavioral consultations. Help may include behavior modification, obedience training, exercise, diet changes, crate training, desensitization, leadership exercises, or drug therapy—all strategies that will be covered in *Dog to Dog Communication.*

What follows in these chapters is how I got Brody and hundreds of other dogs to be better with canines. This book includes photographs on reading dog body language, which will show you how to understand what your dog is saying, whether he is "talking" to you or talking to other dogs. You can learn when he is happy, scared, sad, or relaxed. You can learn when your dog might not get along with another dog and what to do about it. You will learn how to ascertain if you have a dog park dog—a super friendly dog. Or a spirited dog—one that gets along with some dogs but not others, or doesn't do well during greetings, but then is fine with other dogs. And you will get help if you have a very dog-aggressive dog.

What kind of dog do you have? And what is he saying when he wags his tail or curls his lips or jumps on another dog? Is it play or is a fight about to break out? You're probably filled with lots of questions and even more concerns, but now you can finally stop stressing. After reading *Dog to Dog Communication,* your pup will have a better chance of being the talk of the dog park in no time.

—**Jamie Shaw**
Founder of The Dog School

Dog to Dog
Communication

Understanding dog to dog communication
is essential for all dog caretakers.
Credit: Detlev Hundsdoerfer

Chapter 1 Dogs Are Not Born Understanding English

Dogs are not born understanding English. If there was one thing I could teach all dog owners, it might be just that. We, as humans, grow up speaking the language we hear in our homes. If your parents spoke English, then you grew up speaking English simply because you heard the words spoken in your house.

Dogs use body language as their primary form of communication. *Credit: Detlev Hundsdoerfer*

Dogs, no matter how long they hear our words, will *never* understand English simply by hearing it spoken in the home. You can talk to them forever and they will not understand a word we speak. Humans strive to use language to communicate. It's innate in our being. We use other types of communication, like body language, but they are not our primary means of communication. The spoken word sets us apart from other animals. It is unique to humans, and we forget that other species do not use the spoken word as their primary means of communication.

The Importance of Early Socialization

Dogs use body language as their primary form of communication. They also use vocalizations, but to a much lesser extent. Dog to dog communication begins shortly after the puppies are born. During the first two weeks of age, known as the neonatal period, puppies cannot see or hear and their interactions with each other and their mother primarily consist of keeping warm and feeding. The imprinting of pup to mother is one of the strongest actions occurring in conjunction with nursing. The most important development during this time is the relationship bond between mother and pup.

The transition period, which begins around thirteen days of age, starts when the puppies open their eyes. At this point the puppies still cannot see well, but they do respond to light. (They will be able to see completely at approximately five to eight weeks of age, although interactions with each other occur a few weeks earlier.) During the transitional period, which lasts until four weeks of age, puppies will begin to wag their tails, growl, bark, and interact with each other. Play fighting begins at this age.

According to expert dog authors John Paul Scott and John L. Fuller in their book *Genetics and the Social Behavior of the Dog*, it is interesting to note that puppies that are raised in isolation from other puppies or dogs until sixteen weeks of age will never have normal social skills with dogs. They may coexist alongside other dogs, but they will never interact properly. They won't play and they don't express typical body language displayed by socialized dogs.

During this transitional period and into the socialization period, puppies learn most of the communications they need to coexist with others of their species. Through normal day to day interactions they learn to "speak dog." All puppies, unless they are singletons, will learn some amount of social interaction at this point in their lives. As you will see, this can go awry because of breed differences or other causes, but all pups will learn something from their littermates. What they learn during these periods sets the stage for later dog to dog communication.

Genetics can also play a role in this behavior, and some puppies are genetically predisposed to have issues with other dogs—some because their ancestors were bred to fight and others because they are fearful or they are the bullies in their litters. All sorts of things can cause miscommunication, from a traumatic experience to a lack of socialization, and those will be discussed in more detail later on. But remember that all puppies learn something about being with other dogs during this period. These skills and impressions will usually last a lifetime. That's why it's *essential* to make sure your pup interacts with other dogs at a young age. You only have until sixteen weeks of age to lay the foundation for good social skills with other dogs—and then that doggie door swings shut. Luckily, if your dog is older, or you know he wasn't properly socialized as a puppy, there are ways to manage his aggression.

Up until four months of age, pups are like sponges and will acclimate to and accept almost anything to which they are exposed. During these first several weeks of life, you must expose your puppy to everything from men with beards to children on bicycles. If you want your adult dog to be good with babies, now is the time for your puppy to meet them. People wearing big coats with hats and mittens, umbrellas, elevators, car rides, cats, horses, toddlers, teenagers; whatever will be in your life within the dogs lifetime, you must expose your puppy to it now. Once the pup reaches sixteen weeks of age, the door for socialization closes. People ask me, "Can't you get the dog used to something it wasn't exposed to early on?" I tell them a dog owner can show the dog the new stimulus and, with enough repetition, the dog may accept the object on some level but it will never be fully comfortable with it. Dogs don't generalize well. A toddler is not the same thing as a ten year old, and your dog knows this as well as you do.

I teach at the University of Vermont, and a lot of my twenty-something-year-old students own dogs. I know it's hard for some of these students to think about whether or not they will have children—and I'm sure most of them don't factor in how their dogs would act around little kids—because most college students live busy, active lives with a great deal of exposure to various stimuli. However, they rarely come in contact with children. It's just not a part of their lives. College students' dogs are some of the best socialized pups I see, and they tend to have lower levels of aggression than the general population. But they are more inclined to be aggressive with kids because they don't often come in contact with them.

SIDEBARK

Deuce and Laurie

Laurie came to see me with her three-year-old Golden Retriever, Deuce, because she was interested in adding a Corgi puppy to her household. Deuce had not been in contact with many dogs since her time with her litter, and when she had been with them, she was not very well behaved. Sometimes she showed aggression. Laurie wanted to see if she could do anything to make Deuce good with other dogs and, in particular, with this puppy she wanted to buy.

Upon evaluating Deuce I could see she was very dominant with dogs, but luckily still retained some of her social skills from puppyhood. We introduced Deuce to several dogs over the course of an hour, and with each one she became calmer and friendlier. By the time we introduced her to the Corgi puppy, Deuce had regained enough "dog speak" to interact sweetly and with composure with the new puppy. Today, they continue to have a happy life and the dogs play very well together.

Some of these students, however, will go on to have children and their dogs will have to learn to adjust. This was the case for me. When I got Brody and Grace I never expected to have kids in their lifetimes. It just didn't occur to me to think about it. Today I tell my students that if they get a dog now, they should find a way to let it be around children as soon and as much as possible. What you do in those first two months of dog ownership will last a lifetime. And what you don't do during that time period will lay the foundation for a lifetime of trouble if you don't expose your dog to lots of different stimuli. (If you adopt an older dog instead of a puppy, you can know for sure if your dog will be good with others. Evaluate an adult dog with children and other dogs before you choose to adopt it.)

As long as your pup wasn't a singleton, it has had some exposure to other dogs simply by being in its litter. This is fantastic, because some of your work has already been done for you. As long as your puppy had lots of time with its littermates, it has learned good dog skills. Almost innate, dog speak is within all dogs, even those that have issues with other dogs.

During the period of socialization, puppies really learn most of what they need to know about dog to dog behavior. Through this time the mother dog begins to wean her pups, and it may be the first time the puppy is shown any aggressive behavior. At around five weeks of age, the mother may begin to growl at her puppies when they try to nurse. This is a hard lesson, but an important one. They need to learn that if a dog growls, they should back away.

Human interference with a mother dog when she attempts to wean her puppies can cause a great deal of problems for the pups later in life, because they may not have learned the warning signs of aggression. When the mother is weaning the puppies she will advance to more aggressive displays, but she rarely injures a pup.

It is interesting to note that according to Scott and Fuller, the mother's threats toward her offspring can cause fighting amongst the puppies. With most of the breeds they studied this usually was not cause for alarm, except in one terrier breed in which the most submissive pup had to be removed from the litter because of excessively harsh treatment from its littermates. Otherwise, the interactions of the puppies usually led to a hierarchy of submissive and dominant puppies. Careful observation of a litter by the breeder or shelter workers can let a potential owner know what each puppy may be like with dogs later in life based on the order that has been established in the litter (see Chapter 5 for more information).

Also during the period of socialization, play fighting occurs between the pups. Again, this rarely results in any harm but does also help establish the pecking order within the pack. This order or level of submission or dominance can be seen for a lifetime. According to breeder Kathleen Kehoe of Crangold Kennels in

Play fighting is natural between dogs.
Credit: Detlev Hundsdoerfer

Charlotte, Vermont, puppies that were moderate in their play with their littermates will grow up to be equally moderate in their play as adults.

Breeding Golden Retrievers since 1983, Kathleen has seen this over and over again. She says she can usually tell if a puppy is going to be dominant, submissive, or middle of the road with other dogs by the way it acts in the litter, although what the owner does with the puppy can help to make a difference. She gave the example of Stella, a two-year-old female Golden that boards with Kathleen at her kennel. "Stella was the more submissive pup in the litter. When I placed her with her owner, I told the woman that she would need to get Stella out and socialize her with other dogs." Now a therapy dog, Stella will stand still and show submission when she greets Kathleen's other dogs. But after about twenty minutes she warms up and begins to play.

Lastly, during the socialization period some slight sexual behaviors will begin to appear as a few of the pups may start to mount and clasp other puppies. This is usually playful, but mimics adult courtship behaviors. This behavior can sometimes begin as early as three or four weeks of age and continues into all periods of development.

It is during the socialization period that most puppies are taken away from their littermates and moved into permanent homes. This is when we step in as the moderators of their development. It is *so* essential to expose your pup to other pups at this point in its life if you want it to retain any of the skills it learned from its littermates. Frequent play dates with other puppies, a well-run puppy kindergarten class, or time with friends' dogs will suffice, but must be repetitive. If your pup only sees two or three other dogs during the next eight weeks, you will most likely have a lifetime of problems between your dog and other dogs. If you keep your puppy well socialized, it will hopefully have a lifetime of fun play with other canines.

Chapter 2   **Dogs Will Be Dogs:
Breeds, Backgrounds, and Behaviors**

Dog TV. Have you ever spent time watching dogs play? Ever sat in your living room or been to a dog park and watched dogs rough and tumble and enjoy the company of their own kind? If you have, you probably don't need to ask yourself the following question. But if you've never had the joy of observing the complete ecstasy of dog play you might ask: Do dogs have an inherent right to play? I firmly believe "yes" they do. They are pack animals and they should have the right to enjoy conversations with their own species. This does not mean you must own at least two dogs. But it does mean your dog should have the right to greet and meet other dogs.

If you're thinking, *I dunno about that . . .* then try this: Imagine living in a world where you were kept away from all other humans—

where you had no contact with people, ever. The desire to see one, speak with one, just even be *near* one would be huge. Isolation from others is a common form of punishment in prisons. Why? Because it's painful and hard to deal with. And we wonder why our dogs get so crazy at the end of the leash when they see another dog on the street. Your dog is saying, "Hey you, other dog, here I am. See me? I want to talk to you! Where do you live? What's your name?" Your dog craves socialization. This is natural.

Your Dog Is Desperate to Speak to Another Dog

As I said before, dogs are pack animals. If they are dog-friendly, they long for attention from other dogs. They thrive on playtime—tussling, wrestling, noisy fun with another of their own species. Dogs deserve playtime (*if*, and that's a big *if*, they are good at it). If your dog stays socialized as a young dog he will most likely grow up enjoying the company of other dogs. If your dog was kept isolated from other dogs at a young age, it may not enjoy the company of others and so by all means, keep him away from them.

Dogs are pack animals and usually enjoy exploring and wrestling with each other.
Credit: Detlev Hundsdoerfer

Often veterinarians will tell their clients to keep their puppies away from other dogs until they have had a certain number of vaccinations. While this may be important from a medical standpoint, the damage to the developing puppy can be dramatic.

According to Stephen Woodard, VMD, of Waterbury Center, Vermont, one of the difficult recommendations a veterinarian has to make to new puppy owners is how to balance the concern for infectious disease with the need for socialization during the first few months of life. A common recommendation is to keep puppies relatively isolated until the vaccine series is completed. Woodard says he *used* to recommend this but now tells clients that socialization is at least as important as, if not more important than, vaccinations are to having a healthy, happy puppy.

He adds that he has not seen a case of distemper (a viral infectious disease) in more than fifteen years and hasn't seen a case of parvovirus (a severe gastrointestinal disease) in five years. Woodard notes that at least a couple times a month, clients ask questions about behavior issues. Separation anxiety and aggression toward other dogs are the most common. This really should give one cause to wonder which is more important—the isolation until vaccines are complete, or the socialization that is so essential.

"It is my understanding that more dogs are euthanized for bad behavior now than die from these infectious diseases. We may have had epidemics of parvo and distemper in the past, but now we have an epidemic of undesirable and often intolerable behavior. These behaviors are easier to prevent than correct and that is why socialization and training must start at an earlier age," Woodard says.

Woodard suggests that the first thing to do to promote a healthy, well functioning immune system that will be able to fight any infectious organism encountered—not just the few that veterinarians regularly vaccinate for—is to put the dog on a good diet and be sure that he is free of parasites. There are several good commercially prepared dog foods available, but there are many more that are not very good. The better foods contain few, if any, by-product ingredients and no artificial colors or preservatives. The addition of some fresh meats, vegetables, and grains is desirable. If possible, the fresh ingredients should be varied. A fantastic source for information on dog foods is *The Whole Dog Journal*, published by Belvoir Media Group (see References).

As was mentioned, puppies begin to wag their tails and show other interactive behavior at three weeks of age. This is the start of their playtime with other dogs. Usually puppies are kept with their litters until they are roughly seven weeks old. This allows the pups to develop normal play skills. These skills can continue into adulthood *if* they are allowed to continue throughout the juvenile period—at least this is the case for most dogs.

Different Breeds, Different Personalities

Here is where breeds become apparent and make a difference in dog to dog behavior, although there is huge variation within every breed of dog. I have owned three Bulldogs and one of them, Yoda, was pure goodness. He wouldn't have hurt even the tiniest of dogs. And I would really love to tell you that breed differences have no impact on dog behavior, but they do.

Many studies have proven that some breeds of dogs are more aggressive than other breeds.

The fighting breeds, such as any of the "Bull" breeds or Mastiff descendants, often have a hereditary predisposition to aggression toward other dogs. They just can't help it. A dog, such as the Bulldog, which was first bred to hang onto the nose of a bull—and then bred to fight with other dogs—will often retain some of that hereditary nature and not be good with other dogs. This may result in needing to keep your dog away from other dogs in uncontrolled environments such as the dog park.

Management is possible, and with lots of training you can teach your dog to behave in the presence of other dogs. You may not necessarily get him to the point where he will play with others, but he should be able to be around other dogs, or walk down the street, without showing aggression.

Kelley Bollen, MS, owner and director of Animal Alliances, LLC—Companion Animal Behavior Services in Massachusetts, wanted to find out more about dog to dog aggression and

Always pay attention to your dog's body language whenever he is meeting a new dog for the first time. *Credit: Detlev Hundsdoerfer*

to see if there was a correlation between certain breeds and temperament. To do this, she conducted a study that involved temperament testing. Temperament testing is the systematic process of observing how dogs will behave with humans and other dogs under a variety of situations. Modern temperament testing was developed by Sue Sternberg, author and owner of Rondout Valley Kennels in New York State.

Between 2002 and 2004, Bollen temperament-tested all of the dogs that had been surrendered to the Massachusetts Society for the Prevention of Cruelty to Animals in Springfield, Massachusetts. Bollen's study showed that certain breeds of dogs are in fact more aggressive with dogs than others. She learned that dog to dog aggression was most common in the Pit Bull, at an aggression rate of 21 percent of dogs (but this does mean that 79 percent were not aggressive!). The Chow Chow came in second at 16 percent, and the Rottweiler rounded off the top three aggressive breeds at 15 percent. Compare these to the Labrador Retriever, which only showed dog to dog aggression 10 percent of the time (and therefore 90 percent were not aggressive).

Most of us would like to believe that it is all in how the dog is raised, but it's not. Breed predispositions have a big impact on dog to dog behavior. The simple truth is that some breeds may not do well with other dogs. In the magazine *Bully Breeds* (BowTie Magazines, Volume 21, 2002) in an article titled, "You Wanna Get a What!?," Donna Reynolds writes, "Under-

standing this prickly breed trait [dog to dog aggression] is a must for every starry-eyed bully enthusiast. You can't graduate from Bull Breed Reality School until you accept dog-on-dog aggression as fact." Unfortunately some breeds of dogs *are* just more aggressive (with dogs, *not* people) than others, and bull breeds are the most likely to have problems. This is not to say that all bull breeds, which were bred to be great with humans, will have dog to dog aggression, or that all Golden Retrievers will be good with other dogs. You can find dog to dog aggression in any breed, and you can have a very dog-friendly Bull Terrier.

Reynolds goes on to say, "No, your bully breed doesn't necessarily have to have a fighting past in order to throw down with dogs. No, selective breeding for less fight drive has not wiped out this trait. No, the huge help of socializing your dog won't erase its genetics during those intense moments when both dogs want the same Frisbee. Some bullies are much more dog-tolerant and some are closer to their historical fighting roots than others, but each still carries the ancestral voice that whispers, 'Don't push my buttons, Mr. Doggy, or I'll mess with you.' "

There are, however, exceptions and you *must* look at the individual dog. This is where adopting an older dog is wonderful because you can test whether the dog is good with other dogs or not before you bring it home. Tashi is a Pit Bull that was adopted when she was two years old. Owned by my neighbor, Tashi lives peacefully with a pack of six dogs—including three small Jack Russell terriers. I, on the other hand, live with a five-year-old Bulldog, Oscar, and he has been on the human antidepressant Fluoxetine (generic Prozac) ever since he was two years old—the time he started to develop serious aggression toward the other dogs, of all different breeds and sizes, in my house.

I know that Oscar can't help himself. He's not a bad dog; on the contrary, he is human-friendly, playful, and makes us laugh at his Bull-dog antics. But before the help of Fluoxetine he tried to kill my Cairn terrier mix, Wyatt. Anytime Wyatt walked into a room or crossed Oscar's path, Oscar would want to fight. Wyatt couldn't move around the house, come into the kitchen, or jump up and greet us when we got home without Oscar trying to attack him. The use of Fluoxetine has proven very helpful in many dog aggression cases if used in conjunction with training and behavior modification. It's by no means a magic pill, and used alone it won't do much good, but employed along with other management and guidance it can make the difference between a dog you can keep and a dog you can't. If you have a dog-aggressive dog, you may want to discuss this option with your veterinarian. I recommend Fluoxetine in about 20 percent of the aggression cases I see, and I encourage the client's vet to prescribe medication.

So breed differences can matter. A Beagle and a Bloodhound, for example, are both bred to work in packs. Their survival, when the breeds were developed, depended in part on their ability to perform and live with other dogs. An aggressive Beagle would not be tolerated by its hunting owner, who needed the dogs to live and hunt together in groups. The same would be true of a Bloodhound and of count-less other breeds who work together.

Each breed has its unique traits and behav-iors and we will investigate these and how they relate to dog to dog communication. We start with the knowledge that dogs and wolves descended from a common ancestor and all dogs maintain some wolfish behaviors, even though they may be hard to detect. It's not easy to see the wolf in a Chihuahua or a Pug, but even these dogs may circle before they lie down—a common trait among wild canids. Simply give them a bone and you will see the primitive behavior come out. I have yet to meet a dog who doesn't get excited when he's offered a raw, meaty bone.

More importantly, dogs in groups have the same social standards and hierarchies that their wolf predecessors had. Dogs, given the chance, will develop pack mentalities and order as well as pack play, sleeping, and eating behaviors. Dogs that live without other dogs may try to display those pack behaviors with their human family members. This is another reason why proper training is so important to keep order within your human/dog household.

Breed groupings, started by the British Kennel Club in the 1800s, separated dogs based on form and what the breed was bred for—its purpose or function in the human world. There are many ways to divide dog breeds, but they can easily be put into the following categories: gun dogs, scent hounds, sight hounds, terriers, working dogs, herding dogs, and companion or toy dogs. By understanding breed characteristics such as sociability with people and dogs, prey drive, likelihood of getting along with small animals, tendency to resource guard, and so on, you will better understand your dog and how she relates to others of her species.

Dogs develop pack mentalities and will create a hierarchy among themselves if given the chance. *Credit: Detlev Hundsdoerfer*

Gun dogs

Hunting, as seen in the gun dogs, is a behavior that is obviously ingrained in the wolf for survival. While this trait is "watered down" in the dog—so the dog will not kill its prey—it is still reminiscent of the way wolves obtain food. Running in groups, gun dogs have been bred to work closely with their human companions and must be highly trainable so they can point,

flush, or carry prey without killing it. They are hardy animals, often working in brambly brush, cold water, or other harsh conditions. They have soft mouths and gentle natures and often make wonderful family pets, but they need a fair amount of exercise to be happy.

Gun dogs can be loosely divided into pointers, retrievers, setters, and spaniels. Some of the most popular breeds, such as the Golden and Labrador Retrievers, as well as the Cocker or Springer Spaniel and Irish Setter, fall into this category. Because they are bred to work in groups, dog to dog aggression or fighting amongst the pack would not be tolerated. Many gun dogs are dog park dogs!

Scent Hounds

Scent hounds, also bred to work together and not kill their prey, are some of the most lovable dogs on Earth. Driven by their noses and prone to wandering off, they do not do well off leash, but if you have a fenced-in yard or leash-walk your dog, these soft-mouthed, long-eared, mostly short-coated dogs are wonderful companions. They were bred to bark and run down game—requiring stamina and perseverance to complete their job.

Scent hounds don't require direction from their owners, like the gun dogs do, making them less trainable and more distractible. Popular breeds include the infamous Bloodhound, the Beagle, and the Coonhound. Often working in large groups, these dogs should be friendly and amicable with other dogs.

Sight Hounds

Instead of using their noses, sight hounds chase their quarry using their superb vision to guide them. This group includes the fastest of all the dogs and, like the scent hounds, they are usually not good off leash, although they work off leash when hunting. They are long, sleek, agile, and love to run. They require athleticism, and while they enjoy exercise they are content to curl up on the couch like a cat. But beware, the sight hounds were bred to chase and tackle or kill their prey and are not usually trustworthy with small animals, including little dogs. Retired racing Greyhounds, a now popular and sweet-natured, loving pet, must be safely tested with small dogs by introducing them with a fence or baby gate between them or using leashes to prevent any risk of injury, before being placed in a home with one.

I would not recommend a sight hound puppy to someone who wanted to be able to have small dogs or cats also. But, getting an adult sight hound would allow you to determine whether the dog was going to be good with small dogs or cats. Because they hunt in packs, they are usually good with any dogs that are medium size or larger. Common breeds in addition to the Greyhound include the Whippet, the Italian Greyhound, the Afghan Hound and the Saluki.

Terriers

Terriers were also bred to hunt small game and to kill varmints during their work days. Varying in size from the giant Airedale to the tiny Yorkshire these are comical, albeit tenacious, dogs. Given that they were designed to dig out (*terra* is Latin for "earth") and kill animals of their own size, they require stamina and guts. While confident and sometimes independent in nature, most of them are quite trainable dogs. If you have the energy for a fun-loving, funny, vocal dog, they should be good off leash and some are also good at the dog park.

Terriers will not back down if confronted. In fact, they will actually fight back. But like the other hunting dogs, some of them, particularly the smaller ones, were bred to work in groups and some should be good with other dogs, particularly if raised with them. Some, such as the Pit Bulls, may not be good with other dogs due to their fighting heritage. Popular breeds include the Cairn (Toto from *The Wizard of Oz* was a Cairn), Jack Russell, Pit Bull, and West Highland White (Westie) terrier.

Working Group

The working group is characterized by large, strong, determined dogs. They were bred for a variety of activities including guarding livestock and people, pulling carts and sleds, helping fishermen, and participating in search and rescue work.

This menagerie has a large variability in disposition and nature. The sled dogs are independent, long winded, and must work closely with other dogs. Unlike other working dogs, many are terrible off leash. Many of the guarding dogs were bred to chase off other canines and may be aggressive toward other dogs—particularly if not socialized well as puppies or young dogs. But they are trainable and loyal to their owners. The "water" breeds, such as the Newfoundland, are big, goofy, placid dogs. One must look at the original purpose of each breed in this group to know what it will be like with other dogs.

Interestingly, Siberian Huskies, bred to run alongside other dogs, in my experience are often not good with other dogs, especially small ones. In the Novice level of an obedience trial competition, there is a group exercise called the long sit and long down. During this test, the dogs are lined up about two feet apart and the owners are standing about fifty feet away, across from their dog. During the long sit, the dogs are required to stay where they are, in a sitting position, for one minute, and not move at all until their owner returns and tells them they can get up.

I was watching this test at an obedience trial, and in the line-up of dogs were a Husky and a Toy Poodle. After about thirty seconds the Toy Poodle got up and ran quickly toward its owner. The Husky, who up until this point had not moved a muscle, immediately broke out of his stay and started to chase the Toy Poodle out of the obedience ring. Fortunately someone caught the Toy Poodle and the Husky before anyone got hurt, but it did not surprise me that the Husky was the one dog to break its

stay after the Toy Poodle moved. Huskies have a prey drive that makes them not always good with smaller dogs and small animals.

In this group, more than any other, research the original purpose of the breed and then determine what that would imply in relation to other dogs. Common working breeds, in all their complexity, include the Mastiff, Doberman, Great Dane, Rottweiler, Bernese Mountain Dog, and St. Bernard.

Herding Dogs

As the name implies, the herding group does just that—herd! Intelligent, sometimes high-strung, high-energy, and fast, herders are bred to work closely with their owners. These trainable, serious dogs are normally great off leash. They do not make calm house pets, because they require a large amount of daily exercise and a job to do. They excel at dog sports, such as agility, but without a working purpose in life, they will probably be destructive—and they'll bark.

While normally quite good with other dogs, they will sometimes want to round them up, which can incite a fight from the other dog. Ever growing in popularity, the Border Collie was made famous in the movie *Babe*. Border Collies do not make ideal pets. They are brilliant, but require more exercise and training than just about any other breed of dog. They must have a job to do or they will drive you, and all other dogs, absolutely bonkers. Other common herding breeds are the Collie (*Lassie*),

Australian Shepherd (which is actually an American breed), Shetland Sheepdog (Sheltie), and German Shepherd.

Companion and Toy Dogs

Another medley of personalities, the companion and toy group encompasses a variety of breeds. From the Bulldog to the Chihuahua, these dogs are like the working group in that they range in purpose from bull fighter to lap dog—although most were bred for the sole purpose of providing company and companionship.

As with the working group, one must look at the original purpose of the breed to know what the dog will be like with other dogs. If its purpose is to be a warm friend, like the Shih Tzu, then it should be good with other dogs. If, like the adorable Lhasa Apso, whose Tibetan name means "bark lion sentinel dog," the dog was bred to be a tiny guard dog, then it will be less inclined to enjoy the company of other dogs since it was bred to protect against intruders. Usually loyal, spunky, and affectionate, common breeds in this group are the Pug, Miniature Poodle, and Toy Poodle.

People's Reactions to Dog to Dog Behavior

Even when dogs are playing, owners often get concerned. It is hard to know what types of interactions are okay and what behaviors may cause a fight. Throughout the book, there are numerous photos that will help you understand what your dog is saying to another dog. You will learn what is play and what is not. But it's important to look at our feelings about dog talk: How do you personally react when your dog is wrestling with another of its own kind?

Many people get upset when their dogs are talking to another dog. Play includes lots of movement and sometimes, but not always, lots of noise. (When dogs get still and stiff they are moving toward the direction of fighting.) If the play is gentle, sit back, observe, and enjoy the "conversation." Try to learn and understand it. If the play is rough—but still *play*—again, watch, learn, and be thrilled your dog has friends. It can be as important to your dog that she has friends as it is to you. Most humans thrive on some daily contact with other humans. Whether you have coworkers you hang out with, or you spend time chatting with the store clerk when you get your morning coffee, or you have a housemate, most of us enjoy talking to other people. Even if you are not super social or gregarious, you most likely have people you enjoy spending time with.

Doggie friends are a joy to your dog and a great way for her to get much-needed exercise. An hour of dog play is better at tiring her out than two hours of walking on a leash. There is nothing as exhausting for your dog as when she gets to play with her friends. And it should be as happy an occasion for you as it is for her when your dog has a play date.

But what if you have a dog that doesn't get along with others? What if your dog growls, snarls, lunges, or tries to bite other dogs? People get upset when dogs don't get along. It's even worse if the dogs actually break out into a full-out fight. And whether or not you see blood, there's guilt, fear, and days of stressful pondering about what to do with your dog. Clearly, no sane person wants a dog that fights with other dogs. But what I want to do is open people's minds to the idea that most of what we see our dogs do is not that big of a deal. I know that may come off as sounding crazy, and I am not being nonchalant or saying it's acceptable for dogs to hurt each other. *It's not.* But it *is* okay for dogs to have best friends and enemies. It's acceptable for a dog to say, "Get out of my face," or "I don't want to play right now." It's all right for a dog to say, "That's mine," or "I don't feel good," or "I'm having a bad day."

Think about a time when you got mad at your best friend or coworker. Or a day when you fought with your mother or your significant other. After the apologies were said, was it such a big deal? Do you think you'll ever get mad at anyone again? Do you ever swear at a driver on the road or think the waiter at the restaurant is too grumpy? Do you know anyone you don't like even if you don't have a good reason? We make judgments about people all the time. We meet people who we instantly like and those we'll avoid forever. We have best friends. And our bodies and voices express these likes and dislikes all the time.

If you see your closest friend and she runs over to you and gives you a hug, you're proba-bly going to be comfortable with that, right? But if a store clerk randomly did the same thing, it would make most of us feel awkward. We all have a circle of "personal space" around us that we want respected. If someone invades that perimeter, it does not feel good—and we react accordingly.

What's so important about understanding dog to dog aggression is that when our dogs meet other dogs, they are trying to greet them, similarly to how humans greet each other. They are sizing each other up, seeing if they like the way the other dog acts and smells. They are deciding if they want to interact or go the other way. It's we humans who think they should all play gleefully like puppies.

NOTE Some breeds of dogs are devel-oped to be permanently arrested in a juvenile state because they are more emotionally and physically attractive to humans. These breeds are commonly ones with floppy ears and less elongated noses, such as retrievers and spaniels. Many of these breeds are more social with other dogs and will play in a puppy fashion, even as adults. This can really set off dogs that are more mature in their adulthood, potentially causing dog fights. To put it in perspective, it's similar to you meeting an adult who acts like a child. Until you have had the time to understand the difference, this person would appear quite strange to you. You would take the time to get a feel for the person and decide if he was someone you wanted to communicate with.

It should be within acceptable limits if a dog wants to display a variety of body postures toward another dog. You should allow your dog to growl—he's simply sending the other dog a warning to please go away. Every dog displays a wide variety of body language all the time. When dogs meet they are sometimes moving and wagging and sometimes still and stiff. Either behavior is okay, although the stiffness is more indicative of a potential fight than when the dogs are moving around.

I hike with my dogs on a daily basis on my neighbor's land, and my pack often meets up with their pack as we head into the woods. Each day, my Shiloh Shepherd Kobe meets up with my neighbor's white German Shepherd mix, Keisha. They "greet" by charging toward each other and then stopping about twenty feet apart. They stand there for a minute and observe each other. They lean their heads forward and sniff at the air. Then they dance up to each other, give a friendly crotch sniff, and then Kobe turns and comes back to me to go into the woods.

Other dog to dog greetings are less reserved. In my beginner obedience classes at The Dog School we have fifteen minutes of playtime at the start of each class. Most of the dogs come into the class and go running up to the other dogs. They show little to no hesitation. We do first introductions on leash to avoid and prevent problems, but as soon as possible, if possible, we let the dogs run around together. We leave their leashes dragging so if a problem breaks out, we can separate the dogs quickly and safely. Most of the dogs in the beginner class are young and play together like children on a playground. They are eager to get together and interact. Older dogs, like Kobe and Keisha, often show a bit more reservation or distance before greeting each other.

Humans have unfortunately defined a very narrow margin for what is tolerable communication in dogs. We want dogs, like we want children, to be okay together. We have a Disney version of how dogs should act, and that is *not* by showing bad behavior with other dogs. We wouldn't expect a lion not to roar, but we don't want dogs to growl. It's time for people to open their minds to the idea that some displays of communication, or "aggression," are really not so bad.

Accepting Limitations: When Dogs Shouldn't Play

The only way to prevent all dog fights is never to allow your dog to be in the presence of other dogs. If you deem your dog to be seriously dog-aggressive, this may be the only appropriate choice. Many dogs can learn to act properly when interacting with others of their own species. But if your dog can't, it's time to accept that limitation and know you are not a bad owner. As was stated, people get upset and reactive when dogs fight. If your dog isn't just miscommunicating—if he's seriously out to cause harm—you may need to accept that your dog should be kept away from other dogs (see Chapter 7).

Different Kinds of Greeting Behaviors

There are a variety of greeting behaviors that can occur when dogs interact with each other. The four most common ones are: the butt sniff, the head to head greeting, the "T" greeting, and the groin sniff. Within each category a wide variety of body language is displayed along with the initial greeting.

The Butt Sniff

The dog on the left, with her squinty eyes and pulled back ears, is fairly relaxed about the Berner's sniffing. *Credit: Sarah D. Todd*

The dog on the right shows mild submission with her lowered head, tail down, and ears pulled back. *Credit: Sarah D. Todd*

The dog on the left pretends to be very interested in something in the grass (called a "displacement behavior") but is relatively relaxed about this butt sniff. *Credit: Sarah D. Todd*

The dog on the right has an erect tail and her hackles are up as she dominantly butt sniffs the dog on the left. The black dog is uncomfortable but also has a dominant tail. *Credit: Sarah D. Todd*

The dog on the right stands uncomfortably still as the dog on the left sniffs. *Credit: Sarah D. Todd*

The dog on the right is whipping her head around to tell the dog on the left to back off. *Credit: Sarah D. Todd*

Different Kinds of Greeting Behaviors

The Head to Head Greeting

The tongue flick of the Bulldog tells the slightly aroused Bernese Mountain Dog that he (the Bulldog) is not a threat. *Credit: Sarah D. Todd*

Slightly dominant posture on both dogs but otherwise this is a relaxed head to head greeting. *Credit: Sarah D. Todd*

Here is a hesitant but fairly relaxed hello. Notice the low tail on the Shepherd and the ears back on both dogs. *Credit: Sarah D. Todd*

The Shepherd with its forward body posture dominates the alert but unalarmed terrier. *Credit: Sarah D. Todd*

Two dogs confronting one makes the dog on the right uncomfortable. *Credit: Sarah D. Todd*

Notice the tongue flick of the dog on the right as the two dogs stare each other down. *Credit: Sarah D. Todd*

Different Kinds of Greeting Behaviors (continued)

The "T" Greeting

The "T" greeting often has an element of dominance. Notice the head of the dog in back over the black dog who has his hackles raised and tail erect. Both dogs are showing some dominance. *Credit: Sarah D. Todd*

Notice the lowered body posture and hair raised on the lower back of the Shepherd. The Berner stands tall in dominance over the Shepherd. *Credit: Sarah D. Todd*

These two dogs lived together but the one in the foreground still wanted to show his dominance over the Golden. *Credit: Sarah D. Todd*

The dog in the foreground turns its head in deference to the Shepherd who is dominant as is seen by the Shepherd's head over the Border Collie mix. *Credit: Sarah D. Todd*

The Groin Sniff

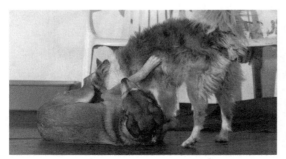

A groin sniff during complete submission. *Credit: Sarah D. Todd*

The dog on the right shows dominance. *Credit: Sarah D. Todd*

Really, it's not your fault. Unless your objective was to teach your dog to fight, you have to understand it's not because of you that this aggression is happening. Lots of things cause dog aggression (see Chapter 3) but few of those factors are human intention. If you determine that your dog should be kept away from other dogs, he can still live a healthy, active, and wonderful life. It's much easier if you have a fenced-in yard, but even if you don't you can learn to teach your dog to be non-reactive in the presence of other dogs. This takes time and training but is attainable for all dogs—from the slowest to the smartest of breeds. As you will see in the next chapter, your dog can even learn to remain calm upon seeing another dog.

If you have a fenced-in yard, you may decide that you don't want to take your dog places unless absolutely necessary. If you provide stimulation and exercise for your dog, he will love you for it. Learn to play games in the yard with him and teach him obedience and tricks for mental stimulation. Fetch is a fantastic way to exercise your house dog. You can play indoors or out, and it is a great way to tire out a dog without you having to do much. This is a super activity for couch potatoes. You can also teach your dog to find hidden objects, play tug-of-war, or do trick training. Tricks are a fun and entertaining way to interact with your canine friend.

If you must walk your dog for him to eliminate, it is much harder to own a dog-aggressive dog. But don't despair, you can teach him to behave while on the street. With some time and effort, you can have your dog walking calmly on leash even if he has to pass another dog. First this must be done at a distance from other dogs (for goodness sake, cross the street!) but eventually you can teach him to walk quietly even when passing another dog on the sidewalk next to him.

I once owned a beautiful Border Collie named Grace. She was one of the most human-aggressive dogs I have ever seen and certainly the most aggressive dog I have ever owned. Grace could be at a perfect heel at my side but then she'd immediately whip her head around to try to reach over and bite an innocent pedestrian who was passing by the two of us. Grace taught me as much about dog to human aggression as Brody did about dog to dog aggression. Grace was not aggressive with other dogs. Grace was a definitely a challenge to own.

For the first nine months of her life I lived in a city without a fenced-in yard. I had to walk her daily to get her to eliminate and I passed people on each walk. It was a terrible time for both of us. I was always nervous she would try to bite someone. People would look at me funny as I reeled Grace in to me and tried to distract her from them. I spent walk after walk crossing the street, trying to avoid people. I cut walks short, went at odd hours, and had to avoid everyone. With her fearfulness of strangers and aggression, walking was a miserable experience for both of us. Grace also went through a transition period of a few years with me during which I went from not knowing how to deal with dog to human aggression to learning to live with it—*and* succeed at having a good life for both of us. I spent countless hours desensitizing Grace to strange people of all ages—first at a distance, then closer and closer. It was through Grace that I learned the most about the process of desensitizing dogs to things that scare them.

Grace's training went so far that she ultimately won several obedience and agility competition titles. She earned her American and Canadian Companion Dog title in obedience and her Novice Agility titles in a few of the U.S. dog agility clubs. She then did a stint as a therapy dog! We made weekly visits with a friend and her Weimaraner to our local hospital and visited patients in the psychiatric wards. I don't know if she really liked being a therapy dog, and in hindsight it might not have been the most fun activity for her, but she did it and never complained. At our therapy dog visits, Grace learned to live for her tennis ball and played fetch for hours with the patients. She even allowed people to pet her, although she didn't prefer it. I was sometimes nervous Grace would have a relapse, but she never did. You, too, can teach your aggressive dog to behave around whatever scares or antagonizes her. It just takes a little learning, some time and patience, and a lot of love.

Chapter 3   Beginning with the Basics

Obedience training opens the door to communicating with your dog. It gives you a chance to teach your dog a very small part of the English language. Remember, all dogs work best with body language, but they are amazing learners and can gain knowledge of a bit of our language and then respond to simple verbal or physical cues in order to perform behaviors we have taught.

Training is a fantastic tool for modifying any behavior in your dog. All of us teach housetraining (eliminating outdoors) as soon as we get a dog. This is essential. Even if you own a small apartment dog and you teach him to eliminate in a litter box or on "pee pee" pads, you're still teaching him to go to the bathroom in a specific location. This is training. Many of us automatically teach simple behaviors such as staying off the counter, keeping out of the trash, sit, or walking on a leash. Many dog owners naturally teach the things that are important to them for the lifestyle they lead with their dogs.

Obedience Training for Good Behavior

Simply put, obedience training is associating a word, such as "sit," or a body gesture, such as a hand held over the dog's head, with an action—in this case, sitting. We call this word or gesture a "cue." It's a verbal or physical signal to the dog to conduct a behavior we have shown him. And the best way to teach a dog to perform these tasks is to use "shaping," which was first discovered in the 1940s and '50s by B. F. Skinner, considered to be perhaps the most celebrated psychologist since Sigmund Freud. Shaping is a method of "successive approximations," or small steps in the right direction, toward a desired behavior.

When shaping, you start by rewarding the first step in the right direction even though that behavior might not look like what you are ultimately trying to achieve. For example, if I am teaching a dog to sit, I will start by rewarding the dog for looking up—not a sit at all, but the primary step in learning to sit. I use a lure, usually food, to show the dog the behavior I want to see from him. I like to use high-quality, small tidbits, either dog jerky treats or small pieces of hot dogs, cheese, or sandwich meats. With some dogs, a toy such as a tennis ball can work, but tasty, small morsels are usually easiest. Most pet supply stores sell high-quality training treats.

In this chapter, we will show you how to teach basic behaviors that are helpful in everyday existence with your dog. More importantly, they are also essential in controlling your dog in the presence of other dogs. Basic training allows you to move your dog comfortably around other dogs, even if he is normally reactive to those dogs. With a simple "Look," "Heel," or "Sit," many dogs can contain themselves—even if they prefer to be barking around other dogs. Your dog can learn to be well-behaved in the presence of other dogs with simple, basic training.

Proper Tools of the Trade

There are only a few things you need to start training your dog. At a minimum, you need a flat buckle or snap-around collar, a leash, and yummy treats like dog jerky treats, hot dog slices, or bits of chicken, cheese, or steak. If you have a dog that pulls a lot when on leash, you may want another option instead of a regular collar to control your dog. The most humane products on the market today are the head halter and the front-attachment harness.

Several brands of head halters are available at most pet supply stores. Get the one that fits your dog best by asking for help from your pet supply retailer. Instructions on how to properly acclimate your dog to wearing her halter are on pages 42–44.

Please note that not all halters come with the best instructions on how to get your dog comfortable wearing them. If you train your dog to use the head halter slowly, she will learn to love the sight and feel of it. If you rush the training, she will resist the head halter and paw at it and rub her face on the ground when you walk her. Take two weeks or more to accustom your dog to wearing the head halter and she will love it for life. Head halters are like power steering. They are well worth the training time it takes to get your dog used to wearing them.

If you have tried a head halter in the past and your dog hated it or you can't stand the idea that a head halter reminds people of a muzzle, you may want to try the front-attachment harness. One of the beautiful things about these new harnesses is that there is no acclimation period. You can easily put this on your dog and he or she usually stops pulling immediately. Often not as effective as the head halter, the front-attachment harness does work well for many dogs. The head halter seems to work better because in controlling the head you can more easily control the whole body. The harnesses work, but not as effectively. If you have a puller on your hands, go to your pet supply store and inquire about these harnesses.

They come in many brand names but all attach the leash over the breast plate of the dog. Most stores will allow you to try one on your dog and walk her around the store or parking lot before you buy it to see if it works. Because your dog doesn't need time to get used to wearing it, you can see right at the store if it's going to be effective for her or not. If it's not effective, then definitely try the head halter.

In addition to the collar, halter, or harness and leash, you need small pieces of tasty treats. The higher quality the treat, the more quickly your dog will learn what you're asking of him. I discourage minimum-wage treats such as crunchy bones and kibble (dog food). Personally, I like to use cut up slices of hot dogs, sandwich meats like roast beef, or small pieces of cheese. If you are adamantly opposed to "people" food, get some high-quality dog jerky treats (available in most pet supply stores). Cut up your treats ahead of time, having them at the ready when you begin your first training session. I like to put my treats in a fanny pack so they are easy to access and deliver when needed.

NOTE Quick delivery of treats is important, and if you have to go digging in your pocket each time you hand your dog a treat, it will be too long between the behavior and the reward. Fast delivery of treats is paramount so the dog associates the cue, hand motion, and food with the behavior you are trying to reward.

General Guidelines for Training Sessions

Another thing you want when training is a dog that is well-exercised. On average, a somewhat tired dog will be able to focus better than a dog that is hyper with energy. Every dog is different and you need to discover for yourself when your dog will work best, but many dogs cannot concentrate on lessons if they have been crated all day. Try various times with your dog to see when he pays the best attention. With some trial and error you will find whether your dog does best when rested or exercised.

Some breeds, like my Bulldog, Oscar, train best after a good nap. But with my Border Collie, Grace, a forty-minute run or ball-chasing session was essential before beginning any training endeavor. Each dog has a different exercise requirement, but the average dog needs a bare minimum of two good twenty-minute exercise sessions *per day* to be able to live a normal, happy life. And "good" means solid activity—running hard, chasing a ball, romping with another dog. Unfortunately, walking on a leash does not provide adequate exercise. If your dog cannot be off leash to run—and few dog-aggressive dogs have a place they can do this—teach your dog to fetch so she can run back and forth even in your house. It's great exercise and does not require you to work up a sweat in the process.

Plan on having two training sessions a day when your dog is physically hungry. Just before a meal is a great time to train. If you are going to train in the morning before work, feed your dog *after* her training session. Same thing in the evening—feed her *after* a training session, not before.

Each training session should last about ten minutes. Like exercise, this is dog dependant. Oscar can concentrate for about five or ten minutes at a time. My Shiloh Shepherd, Kobe, can work for twenty minutes or more at a time without getting bored. The more behaviors you are training per session, the longer you can usually train for. If you are only working on one or two behaviors in a session, you may only want to train for two or three minutes, maybe even less. If you are focusing on several behaviors at one time, you may be able to go longer.

Find a quiet area to begin your training sessions. As your dog learns the behaviors you can add in distractions by going to busier places, but to start you want a peaceful area where both you and your dog can concentrate easily. A room in your house, or somewhere in your yard, is a good place to start. When working on a new step in a behavior, always use your quiet area to train. Once a step is easy, *slowly* add in mild—

then moderate, then great—distractions.

A mild distraction can be something as little as turning on the television. A moderate distraction might be a blowing leaf, and great distractions are people, squirrels and other dogs. As you advance on to distraction training, you can add in rooms of the house, train when there are other people around, or go somewhere new to train your dog. I like to start a new exercise in my house or yard when no one is around. Next I train when someone else is home, and then I move on to training in new locations. When I go to new locations, I start somewhere like a quiet park and then move on to a noisier park or a busy sidewalk. Then when you go on to the next step, go back to your quiet training area to work on that step. As that step becomes easy, add in the distractions: first mild, then moderate, then great. Then, go on to the next step without distractions. Eventually increase the distractions and so on.

You can work on several different behaviors in any one training session. It's actually best if you don't spend too much time on any single behavior at once. Dogs, like humans, get bored. If you spend more then a few minutes on any one exercise your dog will become disinterested and his performance may go downhill. For example, I might work on "look" for one minute, then work on "sit" for one minute, and then "stay" for one minute after that.

When training both Grace and Brody for obedience competitions I would vary the work we did from one exercise to another, never spending more than a few minutes on heel or stay or come. So you can work on Step 1 of each exercise for the first few days or week of training, then move on to Step 2 in the second week, Step 3 in the third week, and so on. You know you are ready to move to Step 2 when Step 1 is easy and fluent. Never rush the steps. Take as long as your dog needs before you move to the next one. You may find you are at Step 2 of one behavior while on Step 3 or Step 4 of another. That's fine. Just advance as your dog is ready. Some exercises will come easily and some will be harder for your dog.

My husband and I used to have a Bulldog named Yoda. Yoda was not at all like most of the Bulldogs I know in that he was perfect with other dogs. We called Yoda "pure goodness." He was an angel of a dog. He always made us laugh, but he was slow. He wasn't just physically slow—you could outrun him—but mentally slow as well.

Having been used to training Brody and Grace, I was accustomed to dogs that caught on pretty quickly. They took to all obedience exercises with ease. Then along came Yoda. I figured if I could put an obedience title on a mixed breed and a Border Collie then I could put one on a Bulldog. So I set to training Yoda for obedience trials. He took to everything with humor but it took a while. What took three weeks to teach Brody or Grace took six weeks to teach Yoda. Everything had to be done in small portions or he would lose interest fast. He would lie down on his sit stay and toddle over to me on his come. I was used to my previous dogs that stayed sitting and ran on the recall exercise. Yoda was a fun dog to train, but I had to shift my expectations. That's normal. Be patient and follow these guidelines to success.

So now you have what you need: an exercised dog, a leash, a collar, head halter or front-attachment harness, a quiet area to train, ten minutes—and the best treats money can buy.

Your Dog's First Words

The first three words you need to choose are your praise word, release word, and stop word. Your praise word tells your dog he is performing a behavior, such as sit or down, correctly. It should be a short, single word that you can say easily and quickly when you want to mark the behavior you're aiming for. I use the word "yes," but I have dog-training friends as well as clients who use "clever," "right," or "excellent." Pick a word you like and can stick with.

To "charge" the word, meaning to teach your dog that something good happens when he hears the word, simply take your dog to his quiet training area with treats such as dog jerky, hot dog slices, or bits of cheese or meat in hand. Say your praise word and quickly give your dog one of the treats. Say the word again and give a treat. Repeat about six or seven times. Congratulations! Your first training session was a success and your dog has learned his praise word! Go ahead and practice the whole thing again later in the day, and even the next day. Repeat this two or three times, and your dog will have it down.

Now it's time to pick a release word. This tells your dog that the behavior you've been working on is over for now. I actually use the word "release," but other trainers and clients use "all done" or "free." I prefer to avoid the word "okay" because it is such a common word and I don't want to accidentally release my dog into traffic or release him at a time I didn't intend. So I recommend you pick a word that is easy to remember but isn't "okay." You will teach this word as you teach your dog's first behaviors below.

Next choose a stop word. This word will tell your dog you don't like his behavior and you want it to stop *now*. I use the word "enough," but others use "stop," or "halt." As with the word "okay," I don't use the word "no" as my stop word because it's such a common word that we use all the time in conversation and to our dogs. So pick a stop word that will be specific to your dog when he is doing something you don't like. Your stop word will be used later in training. You should teach it when you use it by clapping your hands or shaking a tin can with pennies it when you say you say your word. The stop word will also be used if and when you use a spray bottle or breath spray which will be explained later.

Teaching the Basics for Dog to Dog Interactions
Look

A simple and useful behavior, "Look" teaches your dog to look at you, and keep looking at you, until you release her. Start teaching the look in conjunction with the heel, sit, down, and stay.

Step 1. Once you are in your quiet training area, take out one treat and hold it between the thumb and forefinger of one hand. Put your treat hand on your dog's nose and then bring your hand up to the outside edge of one of your eyes. After you've drawn the treat to the side of your eye, quickly bring the treat down to your dog's mouth, say your praise word, and give it to her. Repeat three times. Now, on the fourth repetition, say the word "Look" as you bring the treat from your dog's mouth up to your eye. Remember to quickly give the treat to your dog once you've said "Look" and drawn the treat to your eye, using your praise word each time as well. Repeat three more times, saying "Look" each time you bring the treat to the side of your eye. Good job! Training session number two has been successfully completed!

Step 2. You are now going to increase the amount of time the treat is at your eye while your dog is looking at you. Follow the same guidelines as in Step 1, but this time hold the treat at the side of your eye for five or six seconds before saying your praise word and then giving her the treat. Additionally, say your release word as the treat goes into her mouth (the release word should come after the praise word). This lets her know she can stop looking at you. Repeat several times per training session. Increase the amount of time your dog looks at you, with you holding the treat at your eye, by about five seconds per training session. At the end of a week, your dog should be able to hold eye contact with you for about thirty seconds. If thirty seconds is too long, then go for what you can accomplish and don't worry about taking your time.

Step 3. Now, you are going to transition your dog to look at you without holding the treat at your eye. This is not as hard as it sounds, but it can take a minute or two for your dog to figure out. Remember to be patient with your eager learner. Have a treat ready in either hand, but keep your hands at your sides. Don't worry if your dog is sniffing at your treat hand. Ask your dog to look, and wait. Give her several seconds to make eye contact with you. As soon as she does, say your praise word and give her the treat as you immediately say your release word. If, after ten or fifteen seconds, she has not looked at you, repeat the cue word, "Look," and wait again. If she still does not look at you, go back to Step 2 for a few days and then try again. If you do that and try Step 3 again, she should look at you when you ask. But, if she still won't look when you give the verbal cue, try making kissy noises after you say, "Look." That should get her to make eye contact with you and then you can say your praise word, release, and give the treat.

Once she is looking at you with your hands at your sides, increase the time she can do that up to thirty seconds, extending the time a little during each training session. Great! Now your dog can look for thirty seconds with your hands at your sides.

Step 4. Add movement to the look exercise. Have a treat ready and ask your dog to look. When she looks, wait a few seconds and then take a small step to the right. Hopefully she will maintain the eye contact and if she does, immediately say your praise word, then release word, then give the treat. If she looked away when you stepped to the right, try it again, using both the verbal cue and the hand signal of drawing your hand up to your eye. Repeat three times. Then do the same thing, but take a small step to the left. Repeat that three times. Do this step for a few days or until it's really easy for your dog to get the hang of the exercise.

Step 5. Begin as you did in Step 4 but now, after you step to the right, step to the *left* before you say your praise word and release word, and give the treat. Increase your steps right and left until your dog can maintain eye contact while you step back and forth a few times. For fun, try stepping back away from your dog and then toward her again just to mix it up. How did she do? All of this will increase the amount of time your dog looks and it will increase her ability to do so while you are in motion.

Step 6. There's one more thing to do before we add real motion to this exercise. Today, start by asking your dog to sit and then position yourself so she is directly at your right or left side. Now ask her to look. This should be easy, but if it's not, use your physical cue of drawing your hand up to the side of your eye as you did in the earlier steps. After she's looked at you, say your praise word and your release word, and give the treat. Repeat several times, slowly increasing the amount of time your dog maintains the eye contact to about fifteen or twenty seconds.

Step 7. Hopefully, you've been working on the heel exercise (below) simultaneously to the look exercise. If so, and if your heeling is going well, it's time to put the two behaviors together. Have your dog at either your right or left side and ask her to look. When she does, take one step forward, saying "Heel" *before* you give the praise word, the release word, and finally the treat. If she maintains eye contact, have a little party with your dog because that's a hard step and she's just accomplished it. Congratulations!

However, if you try this a few times and she can't maintain the eye contact as you move forward, go back to using the hand cue of drawing your hand up to the side of your eye. Either way, repeat this three times. Practice both walking to the right side and to the left side with the look command, but just take one step before handing your dog the treat.

Step 8. Now comes the *real* walking. Position your dog at your side, ask her to look, say "Heel," and walk forward two steps. If she maintains eye contact, say your praise word, then release word, and give her the treat. Practice on both the right and left sides. When she can succeed at this, take three steps before the treat. Repeat. Next, *slowly* increase the steps you take—one at a time—until your dog can maintain eye contact and heel for as far as you want. Practice making turns to the right and left, and also try turning around and going the other way (as though you were trying to get away from another dog walking down the street).

Congratulations, you have successfully taught the complete look behavior. Well done!

Sit

As this behavior is often taught by people when they first acquire a dog, your dog may know sit already. If he does, simply practice it until he sits quickly—even in the face of great distraction. Practice in the park, on walks, in the kitchen while food is cooking, anywhere you frequently go with your dog. If your dog doesn't know how to sit, follow the steps below to teach it.

Remember, start in your quiet area—either the same one or a new one, as long as it's quiet and distraction free. Work on Step 1 until it's well done, then move to a distracting area, still working on Step 1—you always want to go from low to high distraction, staying at the same step as you advance in the distraction level. Then move on to the next step while decreasing your distraction level. When you go on to Step 2, go back to your quiet area, and then slowly add in distractions such as another person in the room, the television on, new smells in the air, and so on.

Step 1. Put a small, tasty treat in one hand and place it on the end of your dog's nose. Slowly move your hand upward, causing him to tip his head back. Say your praise word and give him the treat. Repeat three times.

Step 2. Put several treats in one hand. Practice delivering treats to your dog, one at a time, by pushing the treat out between your thumb and the outside of your forefinger. This can take some trial and error, and if it doesn't work you can keep several treats in one hand and give them to the dog with the other hand. Either way, put your treat hand on the tip of your dog's nose and start moving your hand upward. Keep moving your hand up and back and give treats as you move your hand. If your dog is following your hand, give the treat. If your dog ignores you or doesn't follow your hand, don't give the treat and go back to Step 1. Eventually your dog's head should go back far enough to cause his rear end to move into a sit. Repeat three times.

Step 3. Do the same thing as Step 2, but now it should only take a few treats for your dog to fall into the sit position. Repeat until your dog can sit with one treat. When this happens, say the word "Sit" as your dog's rear

end starts falling into the sit position. Repeat several times.

Step 4. The only change here is to start saying the cue word earlier—once your hand is on the tip of your dog's nose but *before* you begin to move it backwards. Say, "Sit," move your hand up and back, and when he sits say your praise word and give the treat. Right after giving the treat, say your release word. Repeat three or four times. Once this is easy, practice the sit command in all kinds of commotion, as mentioned above.

Most dogs take to the sit quite quickly, but occasionally it can take some time. Don't despair if your dog doesn't get it right away. Once I was working with a retired racing Greyhound and it took her a long time to learn to sit. Being accustomed to standing, Greyhounds don't sit easily. I was in a consult with Nellie, a brindle and white four-year-old Greyhound, and her owner, Lee. We spent ten minutes or more trying to get Nellie to sit. Every time Lee held the treat over Nellie's head, she backed up. She would tip her head up but she wouldn't move her butt in the right direction. We finally backed Nellie into the corner, using treats to do it, and when she was in the corner, she finally tipped her head up and put her back end on the ground. It took a while but it was a great triumph when she finally got the sit.

You've done it! Another behavior taught to your dog. Good job!

Down

This can be a bit harder than look or sit, but with some practice your dog will be throwing herself to the ground in order to get that treat. It can be helpful to train this behavior on a slippery floor surface, such as linoleum or hardwood, so the dog's paws can slide easily.

Step 1. Start by asking your dog to sit, give her a treat for sitting, and then put several more treats in your hand. Place your hand on the end of your dog's nose. Slowly start to move the treat straight down from your dog's nose to between her front feet. As you begin to move your hand down, treat. Move your hand a bit more and treat again. As you move your hand from her nose to her toes, treat, treat, treat. Your dog may stand up at some point. This is normal. Just ask for a sit, give a treat for the sit, and start again. Repeat until your dog is comfortably touching her nose to the floor while remaining in the sit position.

Step 2. Put several treats in your hand and begin with Step 1. Once your hand is on the floor, slowly slide your hand toward you, away from your dog. Treat several times as you draw your hand away from your dog, still keeping your hand on the floor. Your dog should move one front paw forward, and then the other, until she is all the way down. If she stands up, don't worry, just go back to the sit and start again. Repeat this several times until she goes down.

NOTE Down often takes longer to teach than the sit or the look. In my beginner classes, we teach the down in the second week of class. We like to demonstrate each exercise in front of the class so the clients can see what to do with their dog. It can often take several minutes to successfully get a dog to go down when we are demonstrating this behavior. As stated, dogs often stand up repeatedly before going down.

In one of my previous consults, Julie brought her male Rottweiler in for help with cat chasing in her home. Van had been living with Julie for only a few weeks when they came to see me. Julie had already fallen in love with Van, but was struggling with Van's chasing her two cats.

One of the things I suggest for cat chasing is to teach your dog to hold a very solid down-stay. Julie had taken classes with previous dogs and had tried to teach Van to lie down but was completely unsuccessful. After spending more than half an hour getting to know Van, I attempted the down. I had to treat, treat, treat, what seemed like one hundred times, just for Van putting his nose to his toes before I could get any forward movement of his paws. He really didn't want to lie down. But after many minutes and numerous treats, Van finally started to understand that he had to put his nose on the floor and keep his butt on the ground at the same time in order to keep getting the treats. I was then finally able to slide my hand forward and get Van to move his legs out in front of him, ultimately going into the down position.

Step 3. With a few treats in your hand, repeat Steps 1 and 2 together, but giving fewer treats. After several repetitions, your dog should be going down with one or two treats. Once this happens, begin to say "Down" as your dog is going down.

Step 4. By now you should be able to do the sit and down with two or three treats. When doing the down, say "Down" just before you make the hand cue, then do the down, then say your praise word, and give the treat. Now release.

Soon enough, you'll have taught your dog the down behavior. Super!

Stay

It is essential that you take your time when teaching the stay exercise. The first concept of the stay that you want your dog to understand is simply sitting still. Increased time and increased distance come with patience. Go slow and you will build a very solid stay behavior. At all steps in the stay, if your dog gets up at any time, ignore him for a few seconds then try again. Also, once your stay increases to thirty seconds, you only want to practice one or two stays at a time because they take time and get long for the dog. Intersperse other exercises such as sit, down, or look in between the stay lessons.

Step 1. Have your dog sit, give him a treat, and stand directly in front of him. Put a treat in one hand and hold it on your dog's nose. Count to three in your head, and while you are counting, tell your dog how clever he is (not your praise word, just "Good boy" or something along those lines). After a count of three, give the treat but put another treat in your hand and count to three again—continuing to tell him how wonderful he is. When it's been a total of six seconds, give the second treat. Repeat again for three more seconds, then say your praise word and give the treat. Now say your release word. If all goes as planned, your dog has just done his first nine-second stay. Good for you! Repeat all of this four more times. After you've released your dog, say nothing to him until you repeat the exercise. This will encourage him to sit still. The praise should come *while* he's staying, not afterward. Remember, if your dog gets up at any time during the stay, stop praising and ignore him for a few seconds, then try again.

Repeat this same exercise with your dog in a down. When he can comfortably sit-stay and down-stay for nine seconds, move on to Step 2.

Step 2. Have your dog sit, and stand directly in front of him with a treat in one hand. Give the verbal and physical cue for stay. The physical cue is holding your hand out in front of your dog's face like a police officer stopping traffic. Do this as you say "Stay." Repeat the exact same thing as Step 1, counting to three while praising and then giving the treat. All you want to do differently is repeat the three-second treating a growing number of times. Do this in *slowly* increasing increments (a twelve-second stay with a praise and release, then a fifteen-second stay with a praise and release, then an eighteen-second stay . . .) until your dog is holding a thirty-second stay with treats every three seconds.

Only give the verbal and physical cue once at the beginning of the exercise. It's okay to praise your dog while he is staying, but as above, withhold praise once you've released your dog. Practice with both sits and downs.

Step 3. During the first two steps you probably had to keep your hand directly in front of your dog's nose when you were working on the stay. To move toward having your hands at your sides, begin as in Step 2, but while your dog is sitting or lying down, quickly pull your hands to your sides and then—just as quickly—put them back in front of your dog's nose. Do this fast motion several times while you are doing the thirty-second stay. With every few repetitions, keep your hands at your sides a little bit longer until you can leave your hands at your sides for the whole thirty-second stay, continuing to give the treat every three seconds.

Step 4. Now you are going to increase the time between treats. Start with the sit or down and cue your dog to stay. This time, count to four between giving treats, going up to a total of thirty seconds. When that's easy, count to five between giving treats again, doing a total of thirty seconds. Then count to six between treats, and then seven and eight, and so on.

Slowly try to work your way up to thirty seconds between treats. It's still okay to verbally praise your dog while he's staying. Practice both sit-stays and down-stays.

Step 5. Through all of this, you have been standing directly in front of your dog while he holds the stay. Now it's time to begin adding distance. Note that this may be hard for your dog because he is used to you being still and close. Start in either a sit or down and ask your dog to stay. After a few seconds, take one step backward away from your dog. Praise him as you move, and if you need to, repeat the cue to stay. Wait for a total of thirty seconds and then *step back directly in front of your dog*, say your praise word, give the treat, and release. When this is easy, go on to Step 6. Remember, if your dog gets up at any time, ignore him for a few seconds and then try again.

Step 6. Time to add more distance. Repeat Step 5, but try taking two steps back from your dog. *Always go back to your dog* before you say your praise word, give the treat, and release. After a few repetitions, try stepping three paces away from your dog. Keep the stay for a total of thirty seconds. Just to mix it up, you can also try stepping to the right and left of your dog, not just straight back.

Step 7. By now you should have a very solid thirty-second stay with you about ten feet away from your dog. For purposes of dog to dog communication, it is a good idea to increase the duration of the stay to a minute or more. This is an easy process. All you have to do is *slowly* increase the amount of time you ask your dog to stay before you give him a treat. Do a thirty-five-second stay, follow with saying your praise word, then give the treat and say your release word. Repeat a few times throughout the day. Eventually work your way up to waiting sixty seconds before giving your dog the treat.

NOTE Remember, if your dog gets up at any time during this exercise, simply ignore him for a few seconds and begin again. Challenge your dog and see what is the longest amount of time you can get him to stay.

Step 8. Working from your one-minute, ten-foot stay, it's up to you how far away and for how long you want to continue on the stay. For purposes of dog to dog communication, a good, solid minute at ten feet away is plenty. But if you want to increase more, simply do so *slowly*. If you move farther away from your dog, add about one foot per stay. In the Novice level of obedience, competition dogs must hold a one-minute sit-stay and a three-minute down-stay while the owner is forty to fifty feet away. Before I had a child, all my dogs could perform this exercise. Then life got in the way (go figure) and the stays my dogs do are much closer to me and a much shorter amount of time. You have to practice as much as your free time in your

life allows. My dogs were much better trained before I got busy with a husband, child, and thriving business. Know that there are no rights or wrongs here. Do what you need to do in order to be happy with your dog.

Heel

A relatively easy exercise to train, the heel teaches your dog to walk at your side. Traditionally practiced with your dog at your left side, I encourage you to guide your dog through this exercise at both your right and left sides. This way, you can put as much space as possible between your dog and another dog on a sidewalk or trail if need be. If someone is passing you on your left, it's better to have your dog heeling on your right. This makes more space between your dog and the other dog.

Step 1. Have your dog sit and give her a treat. Position yourself so your dog is at your right side. Take out another treat and place it on your dog's nose. Make kissy noises or otherwise encourage your dog to move as you step forward. Take three paces and stop. Give your dog the treat. Repeat three times.

Step 2. Have your dog sit and give her a treat. Position her at your left side and repeat the process as in Step 1. Repeat three times with your dog on your left.

Step 3. Have your dog sit and position yourself with your dog at your right side. With a treat in your hand, and that hand on her nose, say, "Heel" as you step forward. Take three paces and stop. Say "Sit" (and wait for her to sit), recite your praise word, and give the treat as you say your release word. Repeat three times. Follow up by doing the same thing with her on your left.

Step 4. Time to add more paces to your heel. Position yourself with your dog at your right side, say "Heel," and begin walking. Take six or seven steps forward, stop, say "Sit" (wait for her to sit), and say your praise word, give the treat, and release. Repeat three times; then repeat with your dog on your left. It is not imperative that your dog heel on both sides, just helpful, so don't worry if your dog prefers one side.

Step 5. Repeat Step 4 exactly the same way except take ten paces forward before the sit. Practice with your dog on both the right and left sides. Then do it again with fifteen steps—then twenty, and so on. Once you've built up to thirty or forty paces, go on to Step 6.

Step 6. Now it's time to add turns. Start heeling. After about ten paces, with the treat on your dog's nose, say her name to get her attention, and then immediately turn to the right. Make the turn and keep heeling for a few more paces before you stop for the sit, praise word, treat, and release. Turns can be random or can be made at the end of a street or up a driveway. Try again, turning to the left. Do this

with the dog on both your right and left sides for several repetitions, but stop before your dog gets bored—maybe a few minutes of heeling at a time

Step 7. About-turns are next. Start by heeling forward. After a few paces, say your dog's name and then turn around and go the other way. Repeat a few times and then practice on your other side. Grace, my Border Collie, was amazing at heeling. I needed her to be so good at it because if she wasn't heeling when we went down a sidewalk, she was free to bite someone. She got to the point where she could anticipate my about-turns and often made the complete turn just ahead of me. In obedience competition, dogs must heel exactly in line with your left hip. Grace's heeling became so perfect (over time) that she never lost points in this part of the competition.

Come

Coming when called is a habit, not a miracle. Learning a new habit takes hundreds or thousands of repetitions. You must practice many successful recalls and slowly increase distractions in order to teach your dog to come when called. Come is necessary for dogs that walk off leash on trails or sidewalks. You may not use it much if your dog is always on leash, but it doesn't hurt to add it to your repertoire of good behaviors. Take your time when teaching this exercise. It's really important to be solid on one step before you move on to another.

Also, the distractions work a bit differently on this behavior. Add in distractions such as new people, smells on the ground, blowing leaves, or a garbage can, as described in the steps below. Practice the come in a safe, enclosed area or on a fifty- to one-hundred-foot rope.

Step 1. While out on a walk, in your yard, or in a large field, reward the dog *every* time it comes back to you for any reason. Just say "Good dog!" or something similar when you give the treat. *Avoid calling your dog to come.* It won't work anyway, and every time you call your dog to come and he ignores you, you undo all of your previous training.

If you need to catch your dog, instead of calling him, squat down and pretend to be very interested in something on the ground. Try going the *opposite* direction your dog is going. Jingle your car keys. *Always* praise your dog when you catch him. *Never* reprimand your dog when he arrives at your side, no matter how frustrated you feel or how long it took you to catch him. Once he gets to you, he's done the right thing and you don't want to show him how mad you are.

Practice Step 1 for a minimum of three days.

Step 2. When your dog is about three or four feet away from you *and moving toward you*, say, "[Your dog's name], come." When he approaches you, say "Good come, good come." Give him a treat *every* time he makes it to you from three or four feet away. The idea is that

SIDEBARK

Dorsey

At my house I have a limited boarding business. I hike with the dogs every day off leash (with the owner's permission) in the woods far away from roads, cars, and people. At the end of the hike all the dogs need to go back into the fenced yard.

One dog I board, Dorsey, a five-year-old Golden Retriever, *loves* to find huge sticks and then play keep-away. At the end of the walk, he is *impossible* to catch. Before I realized this would be a problem, because his owners said I could have him off leash, I would return to my driveway with Dorsey loose with a huge log in his mouth. He would dance around the driveway just out of reach and ignore all my pleas to come to me. I could have the best treats (like hot dogs) in my hand and he wouldn't come to me, staying just out of reach.

It took everything in me not to blow up at Dorsey for his antics. He was having a great time and loved this game. I had to keep my cool and try to figure out a way to get him to come. Luckily I was able to herd Dorsey into my barn, where he became very interested in the pot-bellied pigs. I was able to close the barn door and capture Dorsey. Now when I hike with Dorsey, he drags a thirty-foot rope behind him. This way he can have his freedom to be off leash, but I have control over him when I need him to come.

your dog is already coming to you, and you're attaching a word to that behavior.

Only practice this when you are sure your dog will make it all the way to you. Do Step 2 for a minimum of three days.

Step 3. This step is very similar to Step 2, except that now you want to say, "[Your dog's name], come," when your dog is about six or eight feet away from you *and* committed to going all the way to you. When he gets to you, give the treat as you say your praise word, then say your release word. After two days, increase the distance to ten feet. Do this for two more days.

Step 4. With mild distractions (such as sniffing a leaf, finished getting a drink, or eating grass) and from a maximum distance of ten feet, call your dog to come by saying, "[Your dog's name], come." As soon as your dog looks at you, get *very* excited and praise him verbally as he comes to you. Treat when your dog arrives, saying your praise word and then releasing. Find lots of different mild distractions and keep your distance close to your dog. Do Step 3 for a minimum of seven days. Consistency in training is important, and it's best if you can train daily. But if you have days off in between training days, make sure you do this step for seven days total, even if they are not consecutive.

Step 5. Keep the distractions mild and begin to increase the distance between you and

your dog by a foot a day, using the same guidelines as Step 4. Don't call your dog if he is very distracted. A good guideline is to call your dog only if you would bet $20 that he will come when called. If you don't want to make the bet, don't call your dog. Remember, it won't work anyway and you will untrain your dog if you do this. Do Step 5 for a minimum of seven days as well.

Step 6. You now should be able to call your dog from about twenty feet away with mild distractions. Step 6 requires you to *slowly* increase the distractions while *maintaining* the same, or less, distance. When you are at the base of a tree and your dog is staring intently at a squirrel at the top of the tree, try getting him to turn and come one foot to you. When he is about to roll in something and you are five feet away, call him to come. After he does come, say your praise word, give the treat, and release.

You need to be mindful of what you are trying to get your dog to come away from. If the distraction is too great, you will cause your dog to fail (and this is no fun for either of you). Do Step 6 for a minimum of two weeks. Continue to practice Step 5 while you are doing Step 6.

Step 7. Slowly increase *either* the distance *or* the distraction level when you call your dog. Do not increase both parameters at the same time because it is too hard for the dog.

Kobe

Two of my greatest success stories are with Kobe, my Shiloh Shepherd. One time, my daughter had left a hot dog on the low table in the living room. Kobe, standing twenty-seven inches at the shoulders, was within easy reach of the hot dog. He literally was an inch from having the hot dog in his mouth when I called, "Kobe, come!" and he turned away from the hot dog and came to me. As a reward, I ran to the hot dog and gave it to him—no kidding. I wanted to jackpot the behavior and let him know he had done the best thing in the world by coming to me, and I was going to give him the best reward I possibly could.

Another time Kobe came under great duress was with my neighbor's horses. Kobe *loves* to chase my neighbor's horses, which we pass every day on our way into the woods where we hike. I had been slowly building up the distance and distraction level from which I could call Kobe, but the horses were always beyond his ability to come away from. I would always put him on leash to walk by the horses, or I

would ignore the chasing because the horses didn't care about the dogs and the horse owners weren't bothered by the chasing as their own dogs sometimes chased the horses. One day, after I had been working on the come very diligently, I forgot to put Kobe on leash. Of course, when he got to the horses, he went into chase mode.

Deciding it was time to give it a try I called, "Kobe, come!" and to my amazement, he turned and ran to me. I praised him with all my heart, and when he got to me, I opened my fanny pack and let him eat all the treats that were in there. In the winter, the horses are not in the pasture where I hike, but every spring they are back out and I have to retrain Kobe to come away from them. I do this by backing up in steps and using a long leash if needed. Since I never know when the horses are going to be out in their pasture, I have one day when Kobe gets away with chasing the horses. Then I go back to putting him on leash to prevent the chasing as I re-teach him to come away from this huge distraction.

Make an actual or mental list of everything that distracts your dog, and then rate them from least distracting to most distracting. Slowly, make the distractions from which you call your dog harder and harder. If you try one distraction and it's too hard and he doesn't come, go back a step—or try an easier distraction.

Each time you call your dog, say "[Your dog's name], come." When he gets to you, say your praise word, give the treat, and release. Over a long period of time, your dog should learn to come away from just about anything. Note that it can take about two years to train the perfect come. Just be patient and have fun while you train your dog.

Advanced Training for Dogs with Dog to Dog Issues

Even if your dog has issues with other dogs, it is possible to take your dog out in public. In conjunction with teaching the above obedience exercises, it would be wise to do some desensitization training with your dog. This is not difficult, but does require time and patience. I call this process parking lot training, because much of the work you need to do may be done in the parking lot of almost any store that allows dogs. I recommend you seek out pet supply stores and veterinarians' offices where you can park a distance from the entrance to the store.

To do this training, you need a few items. First you need your dog and a regular, non-retractable leash. I recommend a head halter of some kind if your dog pulls at all on the leash. (Take your time acclimating your dog to the head halter. Don't just put it on right before your first desensitization session. See below.) You also need a small plastic container packed full of peanut butter, cream cheese, liverwurst, or food of similar consistency. Last, buy some concentrated breath spray, which is available near the toothpastes in most grocery stores.

The first thing you are going to do is discover what's called your dog's "critical distance." This is the distance at which your dog is close enough to the other dog to be aware of it, but far enough away from the other dog that he can still eat and he is not barking, growling, or showing any negative behavior. For some dogs, this may be across the street, one hundred feet

away, or forty parking spaces away. Try some different distances until you find where your dog is at his critical distance.

To start, stay at least twenty feet away from the other dog, even if your dog seems comfortable closer in. Your dog may be so food-motivated that he is willing to work close to the stimulus just to get the food. Give him some extra distance to make the training as easy as possible.

My Border Collie, Grace, was so child-aggressive that when we began this training I had to be out of sight of the kids—close enough that she could hear them, but far enough away that she could not see them. And with time, we were able to get to the point where children could pet Grace. So, don't despair: you really *can* train your dog to be close to other dogs without being aggressive.

Now that you know your critical distance, take your peanut butter container (vary what you put in it, sometimes using cream cheese or other pasty things) and your on-leash dog, and go somewhere you will find dogs but can maintain your distance. As I said, I call this parking lot training because I find that going to a pet supply store is a great way to find dogs that are on leash. Stand next to your car with your dog on leash and be ready with the peanut butter.

When you see someone drive in with a dog in the back of the car, get ready. As the person reaches into the back seat of the car to get the dog out, start feeding your dog the peanut butter. Just hold the container at your dog's nose level and let him lick away. Let him lick at the peanut butter the whole time you can see the dog. When the person enters the store with the dog, stop feeding. You want to pair the food with the stranger dog. When the person comes out of the store, start feeding again. Or when another person drives in and takes a dog out of the car, start feeding again. Repeat this each time you see a dog. Spend maybe ten minutes doing this training, or as long as necessary to see about eight or ten dogs, and then put your dog in your car and go on your way.

If your dog is clearly displaying good behavior, you can verbally praise your dog while you are feeding. If your dog is stiff, holding his breath, or growling while eating, this is when you use your concentrated breath spray. Spray your dog right in the nose or the mouth with the spray, using your stop word when you spray. Alternatively, you can move farther away from the other dog, which will decrease your dog's stress level and usually allow you to feed again. If you're not sure, it's best to be quiet and just observe your dog. If you are sure your dog is relaxed and happy, then verbally praise while you are feeding. When you stop feeding (when there is no dog in sight), stop praising. All the good stuff happens while the stranger dog is present.

NOTE Regarding the use of breath spray, I like to say that in a perfect world I would *never* use a correction with a dog. And you can do the desensitization training without any corrections at all. If your dog shows aggression, you can just wait him out and then feed again when he starts behaving. But I find that sometimes it is necessary to communicate to my dog that I don't like what he is doing.

I know that in a strictly doggie world, the growling and lunging are okay. But in my human world, with other dogs in it, it's not always okay to be aggressive. I use the breath spray as the most benign and effective correction I can find. Used sparingly and judiciously, it can let your dog know when he's doing something wrong. Just be sure to go right back to offering the peanut butter container after you've sprayed your dog with the breath spray.

If you are feeding your dog and he does stiffen up or growl, you are too close to the stranger dog. Back away farther, or use the concentrated breath spray. Try adding more parking spaces— or do what you can to make more distance between your dog and the stranger dog. It is also helpful to give your dog a little break between seeing stranger dogs. Move back away from your position in the parking lot and let your dog sniff around or go to the bathroom. If your dog likes to fetch or play tug you can do a bit of this as space and the leash allow (obviously you need to be careful if you are in a parking lot).

If you live in a city and you must walk your dog down a sidewalk where you encounter other dogs every day on your walks, your situation is a bit harder, but you can still be successful. You want the same props: head halter, leash, peanut butter container, and breath spray. When you see the stranger dog, do your best to make more distance. Cross the street if possible. If you can't, then go up onto someone's lawn or stand between parked cars. Once you've made more distance, stand still—this makes the training easier.

Follow the same procedure as above by feeding your dog from the peanut butter container at your dog's nose level as the stranger dog passes your dog. If your dog becomes aggressive and won't eat, either wait him out or spray him. As the stranger dog goes on its way and there is more distance between your dog and the stranger dog, hopefully your dog will calm down enough to start eating. Go ahead and feed him until the stranger dog is out of sight. You can verbally praise your dog if he is eating and is showing signs of being calm such as breathing in a relaxed manner and freely moving his body around. Stiffness accompanies aggression (prefighting) and this is one of the easier things to look for to see if your dog is relaxed.

Putting Parking Lot Training Together with Obedience

Work on your obedience training (as described above in this chapter) separately from the desensitization training. Practice your obedience around various, non-dog distractions before you can expect your dog to look, heel, sit, down, stay, or come in the presence of a stranger dog. Consider other dogs the ultimate in distractions and wait until the behaviors are well learned before adding in dogs as a distraction.

As I described in the introduction, my dog Brody was very aggressive with other dogs. At class he would lunge, bark, and growl at other dogs. I began the desensitization training many years after I had begun obedience training, but when I put the two together I was able to go on to win at obedience competitions with him. And in the Open level of competition, dogs are required not only to heel off leash with other dogs around, they have to do a three-minute sit-stay and a five-minute down-stay with their owners *out of sight!*

When I first began training Brody for this I was a nervous wreck, worried about what he would do if he got up from the stay. But as time went on and he performed beautifully, I gained confidence that Brody would not only hold his stay but behave himself if he did get up during the exercise. Another amazing thing Brody did was lie under a table at my obedience classes, calm as could be. He would just stay under the table, off leash, and watch all the other dogs do their exercises. He was a very good boy!

Training Your Dog to Wear a Head Halter Collar

The training process to help your dog grow accustomed to wearing a head halter collar takes about two weeks, and with continued reinforcement your dog will learn to love the halter as much as she loves the leash. If done slowly enough, at the end of the training period your dog should be comfortable wearing the halter whenever you attach the leash. Use the head halter for any dog that pulls on leash or needs desensitization training. You can purchase head halters in most any pet supply store.

Day 1

Touch the halter to your dog's face while feeding treats for two or three seconds. Repeat this exercise throughout the day, advancing to slipping the nose section of the halter over your dog's nose and *instantly* taking it off. Always feed treats while the halter is in contact with your dog's face.

Days 2 and 3

Prepare your dog's food and put the bowl on the counter. Snap the halter onto your dog's face and immediately feed your dog. Take off the halter as soon as your dog finishes eating. Ideally, this will give you two quick training sessions. Additionally, find two other times during the day to practice with your dog. In those sessions, put the halter on and feed your dog treats for one minute. As soon as you stop treating, take off the halter. It is important to take the halter off *before* your dog has a chance to paw at it. If you find that your dog does paw at the halter, leave it on until he stops. Then quickly reward and remove the halter. Do not attach the leash at any time during these days of training.

Days 4 to 6

Now that your dog is used to wearing the halter for short periods of time, you are going to extend the time the halter is on. Before preparing your dog's meal, put the halter on him. Give a treat, praise, and keep his attention so he doesn't paw at the halter. Feed your dog. After the meal, keep the halter on for another two to three minutes. If your dog starts to rub his head, get his attention back and refocus him on you. Reward him when he is not bothering the halter, and then take it off. Continue with two additional training sessions per day, and put the halter on before you prepare the treats. Feed treats for one minute, leave the halter on for two to three minutes more, and then remove it. As with meal time, if he paws at the halter, refocus him on you and only remove the halter when he's not bothering it.

Days 7 and 8

Continue similarly to Days 4 to 6, but slowly extend the amount of time the halter is on your dog both before and after feeding or treating. In addition to this, add in another training session during which something exciting happens while the halter is on. For example, put on the halter and then hike your dog off leash, let him play with another dog, or play fetch. Praise and treat your dog periodically while the halter is on as long as he is not pawing at it. If he is, see above. Allow the halter to be on for up to thirty minutes.

Days 9 to 12

When feeding your dog and doing the treat-training sessions, attach the leash to the halter so your dog gets used to feeling the weight of it.

Continue to put the halter on your dog when he is distracted with something "fun" (now up to forty-five minutes). Also, practice walking your dog on leash while he's wearing the halter but not having the leash attached to the halter. Keep the leash attached to your dog's regular buckle or snap collar.

Days 13 and 14

Start attaching the leash to the halter and walking your dog on it for short increments. Switch back and forth between the halter and the regular collar, not pushing your dog or you will need to back up several steps. Continue to have your dog wear the halter during feeding and while doing his "fun" activities (up to one hour).

Slowly increase the duration you use the halter until it can be used for the entire walk. Some dogs respond quickly and happily to the halter, and others take longer to train to wear it comfortably. If you feel this guide moves too fast for your pup, simply go slower. It's okay to take three or four weeks to train your dog to be comfortable in the halter.

Chapter 4   What Kind of Dog Do You Have?

Good communication can be as fluid as water flowing in a stream. When your dog plays well with another, she shows grace and agility along with, possibly, gregariousness. There is smoothness to her movements and she is having as much fun as you would have in a water park with a child. Happy, healthy com-munication is a result of heredity and socialization, as I've stated.

Dogs communicate with each other for a variety of reasons, from sheer play to chasing game. As with wolves, communication maintains a steady social structure, resulting in many benefits to the whole pack. Communication

The "play bow" is a classic invitation to play! See how the Golden in the middle play bows to the Border Collie. *Credit: Detlev Hundsdoerfer*

The Leonberger mix puppy bows to the smaller dog. *Credit: Detlev Hundsdoerfer*

makes it possible for the wild pack to secure food and breeding rights. While these things are controlled by humans for the domestic dog, pack order is still essential and "talking" to each other makes this pack order possible. If there is a lack of communication or too many miscommunications, groups of dogs are guaranteed to fight.

The Pecking Order of the Pack

It is interesting to note that the most dominant dog fights the *least*. It's the middle-ranking members who have the most frequent struggles, never quite settling into their place in the pack. The alpha and the most submissive dogs have it easier in many respects. The highest ranking member asserts himself subtly and rarely needs to display hostile behavior, often only fighting in the rare cases when his status is questioned. The "underdog" also rarely fights, demonstrating her rank in constant submissive behaviors. In all household packs there will be an order that is hopefully copacetic.

Even at the dog park where the pack is always changing, there is a hierarchy. If the dogs are doing a good job talking, listening, and respecting each other, all is well. But sometimes communication goes awry and we end up with miscommunication or even aggression.

I met with a friend, Liz, who owns a twenty-one-month-old Bouvier des Flandres named Dickens. We wanted to take a hike together with our dogs. I had only brought Jigs with me, want-

ing it to be an easy and carefree time for both the dogs. I let Jigs out of the car at Dickens's house and unfortunately, Dickens ran over and pounced on Jigs, biting at the back of Jigs's neck. This was not a friendly or peaceful greeting or form of communicating.

Communication, Miscommunication, and Aggression

It is not in the nature of pack animals to want to harm another of their own species. Wolves developed in nature to exist communally. They raise their young together, with aunts and uncles playing an important role in the upbringing of the pups. Often the pack leaders, the mother and father of the young, will go off to hunt and leave other relatives to guard and play with the puppies. Wolves hunt cooperatively with their pack, enabling them to take down animals much larger than themselves. They eat in order of status, with the alpha male and female eating first, but all are allowed to gorge on the kill. Wolves also play together, den together, and move together in a group. They have intense family structures that include a pack hierarchy. Dogs, too, will develop this pack order if living together in groups.

As dogs descended from wolves and became companions of and coworkers with humans, they too, developed a pack mentality and order. Village dogs—as free-ranging dogs of many countries are called—fought for food but also worked and lived together in groups.

Free-ranging dogs in U.S. cities will form packs and live together as well. Overall, it is in the nature of dogs to want to coexist and not harm each other. Therefore, most displays of dog behavior are communication, not aggression. Dogs were simply not originally designed to want to harm one another. This has changed, of course, with human unkindness by breeding, rearing, and teaching some dogs to want to fight with others.

Communication is when one dog is talking well to another—conveying information, revealing something about itself. In a dog-friendly dog, this is a play bow, a groin sniff, a high-pitched bark, an easy wag of the tail. In a tentative dog, it may be a scornful look, a head turn, a holding of one's breath. Think of yourself—you do not have to hit another person to make him understand you are not happy with him. A raised eyebrow or a stare will often do the trick. Think of a time when you wanted someone else to know you were mad at him. You may only need to cock your head to the side, slightly lower your voice, or simply look away to convey your feelings.

Dogs can convey their feelings subtly, too. They have numerous displays of body language that communicate what they are feeling, just as humans do. Look into the eyes of your canine companion and you will see a thousand expressions at one time or another. From funny to happy to scared or sad, your dog can relate these feelings to other dogs more easily than they can be relayed to a human being.

Watch any two dogs of the same breed playing and you will see a style to their play. Not all dogs play the same way. Herding dogs will round each other up, heading the other dog off at every turn. Scent hounds will all put their noses to the ground and go in search of something. Many of the gun dogs wrestle and romp in typical puppy play fashion.

I recently had an obedience class with three Doberman puppies, littermates owned by three different families, in it. The Dobes stuck together and played in their own group while the other dogs played around them. This did not surprise or concern me. They had their own style and enjoyed the company of each other more than the other dogs. Because each breed was designed for a specific purpose, their play styles can vary from breed to breed. Dogs will mix with other breeds—they are not prejudiced—but interbreed playgroups can lead to miscommunication.

Miscommunication happens when there is a breakdown in one dog relaying information to the other. Not all miscommunication is aggression. Miscommunication tends to be most common when different breeds of dogs are relating to each other.

Just the other day, I was hiking with my dogs. With me were Jigs, the newest addition to my dog family, and Annie, a one-year-old Pit Bull boarding with me. I had recently adopted Jigs, an eleven-month-old Border Collie, from Glen Highland Farm in Morris, New York. Annie had been rescued by her owner through an adoption group in Stamford, Connecticut. Jigs and Annie were trying to play with each other. I say *trying* because their play styles were so different that most of what happened was Jigs herding Annie and Annie grabbing at Jigs's front legs. Jigs kept trying to get behind Annie, as Border Collies will do, and Annie, being a Pit Bull, wanted to playfully "bring down" Jigs. They ran through the woods like this, with neither dog being quite satisfied with the interaction but neither dog hurting the other either. I watched them play, never needing to intervene but always keeping an eye on them to be sure it didn't advance to something more than play.

Another cause of different-breed miscommunication is that some breeds of dogs, such as spaniels and retrievers, were bred to remain puppy-like, even into adulthood. This is part of what makes them so lovable to humans. Unfortunately, when you pair a breed like this, such as a retriever, with a dog that is not juvenile as an adult, such as an Alaskan Malamute, it often makes for a mismatch.

It would be like you meeting an adult for the first time who acted like a child. Until you understood that the person was somehow developmentally delayed, you would wonder why this adult-looking person was acting like a kid. In fact, we often say to an adult, "Stop acting like a child." It simply doesn't make sense when an adult person acts childish. Nor does it make sense to one dog when another adult dog acts like a puppy. It confuses the first dog and makes the overtures of the second dog

inappropriate. This will invariably lead to miscommunications.

Causes of Miscommunication and Aggression
Breed

As was discussed previously, certain varieties of dogs have more miscommunications. From my experience in the class I teach for dogs with serious dog to dog aggression issues, I can tell you that some breeds of dogs are more aggressive than others. My personal experience echoes that of animal behavior consultant Kelley Bollen and many other trainers. There is just no getting around the fact.

Heredity

Aggression can be passed down from one generation to the next. If at all possible, a potential new owner should meet both the parents of a prospective puppy. I know this is often not possible, especially if you are rescuing a puppy, but try to meet them if you can. Puppy temperament tests, such as seeing if the pup will retrieve, lifting the puppy off the ground, and calling the puppy to come have proved iffy in revealing adult temperament, although the work of renowned author and shelter owner, Sue Sternberg, may be improving these results.

Upbringing

The way a puppy is raised by its mother will have a huge impact on later behavior. Watching

The pure joy of play! The open mouths show content and relaxed body language. These puppies had a hard but happy play session.
Credit: Detlev Hundsdoerfer

but overcorrection can harm the pup's developing mind.

In his book, *The Dog's Mind*, Bruce Fogle cites the work of Erik Wilsson of the Swedish Dog Training Centre, saying:

When pups tried to suckle, some bitches "punished" their pups with "inhibited bites" more than others did. These pups started to show passive submission by lying on their backs to be licked earlier than other pups. "Growls" and "mouth threats" also led to passive submission. The care dependency relationship had evolved to one of dominance-submission. The severity that the mother uses in altering this relationship has a direct bearing on how that pup will ultimately behave with people. Some of Wilson's "mothers" were extremely aggressive with their youngsters and continued to punish them even after they withdrew from her. Others were more benign, showing less aggression and vigorously grooming the pups afterwards. Wilson says that there were stronger social bonds in these litters and that these mothers were more likely to "paw" their pups into submission. He concluded that pups from litters that had been subjected to a lot of "inhibited bites" were less socially gregarious with people than other pups.

the mom dog with her puppies can be very helpful, because if the mom is overly corrective of her puppies, it can have a lasting impact. Judicious corrections are essential for proper development,

It only stands to reason that these same puppies would be less "socially gregarious" with other dogs, especially because we are talking about dog to dog communication when we look at the bitch-offspring relationship. So, if at all possible, observe the mom with her babies. If you can't be there to watch this, ask the breeder or shelter staff to videotape the interactions in the litter. This may seem like an unusual request, but most people have video cameras and they should be willing to take the photos.

Learned Behavior

What is meant by this is any way a dog may have learned aggression from another dog excluding his upbringing by his mother. As with the mom-puppy relationship, littermate interactions can have a lasting impact in the developing puppy. If you are selecting a puppy from a litter, avoid choosing the pathetic-looking one who sits in the back of the pen and gets picked on by all the other puppies. Also, avoid the puppy that is most dominant with the other pups. Both of these puppies are likely to grow up with problems with other dogs. They learned it early on, in the litter, and that education will last a lifetime.

You might want to think that this early learning can be changed by kind human care and intervention, but it can't be. Yes, socialization will *help*, but it's not always enough to erase the experiences the pup had in its first few weeks of life. This is true regarding the mother's treatment of her puppies, but it's also true of the way the puppies treat each other in the litter. Again, watching the puppies together

is extremely important. This way of thinking helped me to choose Kobe out of a group of puppies. When I picked out Kobe, I spent an entire day watching the mom and the puppies together. The mom was with them for a period of time, and then she was taken out of the room.

Once alone, I spent several hours just observing the puppies play with each other. Kobe was clearly in the middle of the pack—sometimes on top, sometimes on the bottom. He was always chasing and willing to be chased. He played tug-of-war with a toy and was neither so dominant that he always won, nor so submissive that he always lost. He didn't fight when it was feeding time. He was perfectly even-keeled.

If at all possible, spend time with a litter of pups if you are buying or adopting one. If you observe a litter and all the pups are aggressive or overly submissive, as hard as it is, pass on a puppy from that litter and keep looking.

Obviously if you already have your dog or if you are adopting an older dog, this option is not available to you. If you are adopting an older dog, watch it play with other dogs and observe its behavior. If it has good play skills, then you're all right. If it does not play well, then you might want to pass on that dog if you're looking for a dog that is good with others.

Learned aggression does not occur just because of littermate behavior. Your pup may have had an ideal experience with its mom and litter and still develop aggression problems. Adult learned aggression is more likely to happen if you have a multi-dog household, but can develop from any negative interactions between your dog and another dog.

Frequent trips to the dog park are another way your dog might learn to be aggressive. Many dog parks are not well monitored, and I have seen a great deal of inappropriate and harmful behavior at dog parks. Repeated exposure to overly dominant or aggressive dogs can teach your dog to be aggressive. Also, too much submission can backfire on you. Surprisingly,

Submission is a normal part of play. The Rotti puppy "smiles" as she submits in play.
Credit: Detlev Hundsdoerfer

However, submission is also used to communicate with aggressive dogs. The Border Collie's dirty look causes the hound mix to submit.
Credit: Sarah D. Todd

the most submissive of dogs often become the most aggressive because they have been shown so much aggression. Even if your dog has a history of being submissive, being the brunt of aggression too frequently can result in problems.

A one-sided assault or two rarely has a lasting impact on a dog. If you shake it off, your dog is likely to do so as well. If you react strongly, and console your dog extensively, one incident can have a lasting impact. But if you are casual and don't make a big deal out of it, your dog is likely to have no lasting impression from one or two miscommuniations (assuming they are not severe). If an attack is severe, resulting in serious injury, it can permanently change your dog's view of other dogs. Your dog may assume an offensive position every time he sees another dog, and this behavior can become aggression depending on how the other dog reacts to your dog.

Stress

Less common than other forms of aggression, stress can easily trigger a dog's aggression. Sometimes it's difficult for the owner to see that stress is playing into the dog's aggression level when it's at the root of a dog's behavior. As a result, this problem can go on for a long time. While we love when our dog "knows how we're feeling," we don't realize how much our dogs feel and carry our life stresses, too.

Do you find yourself yelling at the kids or arguing with your partner? If so, your dog may pick up and react to that stress by taking it out on another dog in the house or in the neighborhood. I know this from personal experience. Your dog has to find a way to let off steam, and often throws those feelings at another dog. This type of aggression can be less of an issue than other types if you can find a way to alleviate the stress in your dog's life.

Stress-induced aggression does not have one typical physical display, but usually lacks fear and has more components of dominance aggression than other types. If you cannot minimize the stress your dog is feeling by changing the environment where the stress is occurring, you may need to limit the contact your dog has with other dogs until the stress can be removed. Finding a way to minimize the stressors will be beneficial for both your dog and your household.

Stress-induced aggression can also occur when big changes take place in your household or in your life. Did you start a new job and now have a new schedule? Did you have a baby or move to a new location? Any of these types of changes can cause your dog's behavior to transform, and stress-induced aggression can be a result. Usually seen in dogs after puppyhood, this aggression is more common in dogs that are unaccustomed to variability. If you raised your puppy to move around a lot or he's used to changes in your routine, these things are less likely to cause problems. But if your dog has been accustomed to a stable routine and now there is a sudden change, stress-induced aggression may surface.

Try to spend extra time with your dog, and provide more exercise and mental stimulation. Take a class together, such as agility or a tricks and games class. Dogs are quite adaptable, and with time your dog should acclimate to the change and be less bothered by it. Keep your dogs separate within the household if necessary until the stress has passed. Or avoid going to the dog park for a while. Once the stress is alleviated, your dog's behavior should resume to normal within a few weeks.

NOTE Unlike humans, dogs don't understand reassurance. It's a normal human reaction to say, "It's okay, you're fine," when your dog seems upset, but this will actually worsen the behavior you're trying to fix. Next time your dog does something that seems like it warrants reassurance, do nothing. Just observe him. If he starts doing something you like, praise away. But if he is cowering, shaking, putting his tail between his legs, or otherwise acting afraid, say nothing. Watch his body language so you can praise when he overcomes his fear, but say nothing and do not pet him while he is showing fear.

Redirected Aggression

Redirected aggression occurs most commonly in multi-dog households when dog A aggresses upon dog B and then in turn, dog B aggresses upon dog C. In my house, Oscar still goes after Wyatt way too frequently. After the fight is over—and I always have to intervene; you

Common Body Language of an Aggressive Dog

In this series of photos, Xena, a German Shepherd, becomes increasingly aggressive toward another dog on the other side of the fence. Notice how her body posture lowers, her ears flatten, and her teeth come out.

(more photos on next page)

All photos credit: Sarah D. Todd

Common Body Language of an Aggressive Dog *(continued)*

should *see* me trying to get the Bulldog off Wyatt—Wyatt will sometimes turn and go after Jigs, even though Jigs is bigger than Wyatt. Why is this? Wyatt is more dominant in my pack. He is so pent up with anxiety that he turns on the next dog in line and attacks him.

I have seen this happen in dog parks and in classes numerous times. In our obedience classes, we allow closely monitored playtime. But sometimes play can get a bit out of hand when one dog gets too rough or bites too hard. We interrupt this behavior with a squirt bottle filled with water or with a brief time-out if the dogs don't remedy the situation on their own (which is often the case).

The ideal way to manage redirected aggression is to get at the root cause of it and stop that before it begins. If this isn't possible, as in the case of Wyatt and Oscar, watch the dogs around the fighting pair to prevent one dog from redirecting onto another. Redirected aggression can be nasty, and usually has the components of dominance aggression in it. Intervention is always appropriate if one dog is about to redirect on another, but do not coddle the third dog or he will become overly reactive to aggression. Just be matter of fact, separate the two dogs, and go about your day.

Pain and Illness

While it may seem obvious that you would know when your dog is in pain, dogs are extremely good at hiding their discomfort. Being in the sport world with my dogs, I see many dogs at

agility trials that refuse to jump or do a performance obstacle and their owners think the dog
hasn't been trained well enough, is under stress,
or that something else is amiss. Many of these
dogs are actually in pain.

Hidden well, pain causes more aggression
than we know. Why? Because dogs don't complain when things hurt. Without the emotional
content of pain, dogs deal with it much better
than humans. Look at a dog that has been
spayed and watch how within twenty-four
hours, she's up and around and running in the
backyard. The vet will tell you to keep her quiet
for ten days and you will wonder how you are
ever going to do that. When a human has a
comparable surgery, she or he is in bed for days
and not back to work for weeks. (That person
is probably irritable and will complain a lot,
too.) Dogs recover much faster than humans,
but will still react to pain if it is severe enough.

An injured or ill dog may become aggressive with other dogs in the household or at the
dog park, and you should be aware of your
dog's behavior if he's injured. Sometimes in a
multi-dog household it is necessary to isolate
the sick dog to prevent it from being aggressive toward the other dogs. This is safer for all
involved and is hopefully only a temporary
situation. Elderly dogs often become arthritic
or have other ailments that can cause pain, and
changes in the location of dogs may become
needed. Your elderly dog may stop enjoying
contact with other dogs and if this becomes so,
you need to try to provide a quiet space in your

SIDEBARK

Blake and Larry

Blake was a four-year-old, well-muscled,
intact male Rottweiler who came to see me
with his owner, Larry, after he had tried to bite
both a person and a dog in the same day.
Larry, a restaurant owner, had been bringing
Blake to work every day since Blake was a
young puppy.

While Larry worked, Blake was content to
hang out in the office, where staff would
come and go throughout the day and night.
Blake was easygoing and loved everyone at
the restaurant. Blake also had several dog
friends who frequented the restaurant and
accompanied Larry and Blake when they
hiked or went to the park. Blake truly was a
delightful dog with no issues prior to the
past several weeks. Larry reported to me
that Blake loved everyone and had never so
much as hesitated to greet new people and
dogs. He was gentle and loving, and until
recently, had never even growled.

Larry came to see me because about four
weeks prior to our consult, Blake had myste-
riously started to back away from people he
knew. This progressed to growling when
people came into Larry's office, or growling
at the dogs that came in with the visitors.

Larry had taken Blake to the vet, who did
complete blood work and a physical exam.
The blood work and exam showed everything to be normal and Blake was declared a
healthy dog. Larry said Blake showed zero

continued on next page

SIDEBARK

Blake and Larry (continued)

signs of illness, continuing to eat with gusto and always enjoying their outings together. Yet anytime a dog or person got too close to Blake, he backed away, growled, and ultimately tried to bite a human friend and a dog friend in the same day.

As I gathered information, I could find nothing in what Larry told me that would lend itself to this problem. Larry had owned Blake since he was eight weeks old, Blake had been well trained and socialized, and was four years old with no previous signs of aggression. And watching Blake, he seemed like the relaxed dog that Larry described. After I had asked Larry everything I could think of, I decided to try some physical contact with Blake, which I had avoided up to this point because of the attempted bites.

On one of my trips to see Dr. Kurt Kenney, a top veterinary orthopedic specialist who works out of various vet practices in Vermont, he showed me an easy way to see if a dog has any obvious physical discomfort in a few areas of the body. Mind you, I am *not* a vet and do *not* pretend to be one, but I was baffled by Blake's aggressive outbursts and was convinced there had to be a physical cause, even though Larry said Blake had sustained no injuries and showed no illness.

Dr. Kenney had shown me a few things a layperson could do to spot physical ailments in dogs. Slowly, I began to press one finger on either side of Blake's spine beginning at the neck and

moving slowly toward his tail. What I was watching for was a turn of the head toward my hand or Blake holding his breath or some other more obvious sign of discomfort.

Blake seemed to be enjoying this contact until suddenly, as I reached about two-thirds of the way down his back, Blake turned to attack me as though he were Cujo. I moved fast enough and did not get bitten, but it was close! I had not asked Larry to hold Blake's head and I was not prepared when Blake exploded in pain at my touch. I should have been!

There was no question that Blake had been reacting to people and dogs the way he had because he did not want to be touched. It hurt too much! After almost getting bitten, I usually refer clients back to their vet and tell them to specifically ask for an orthopedic work-up in conjunction with the physical exam and blood work. It was a close call with Blake, but I have to admit I was relieved that something was medically wrong with him to explain the aggression. Larry took Blake to see Dr. Kenney, and three days later Blake had surgery on a disk in his back. Larry could never pinpoint what caused the injury to Blake, but it was clear that something must have happened. After his recovery, Blake has never so much as growled again. He returned to his happy, loving self.

house for your old dog. Sometimes an old dog is content to lie quietly behind a gate while the younger ones romp around. Safe space for all is essential.

Above all, if your dog becomes aggressive seemingly out of nowhere, it is vital that you take your dog to your veterinarian and get a complete physical and orthopedic exam, including blood work. Sometimes it is necessary to seek the input of a specialist as is seen in the case of Blake (left).

Diet and Nutrition

Once again, I must state that I am not a veterinarian and I do not pretend to be one, but I have seen changes in food allow changes in a dog's behavior. If your dog is aggressive toward others, you might want to consider trying a dog food with a different main ingredient, such as switching from a beef-based food to a chicken-based food, or from a commercial dog food to a raw food diet.

When Brody first developed dog aggression, he was eating a premium dry dog food with chicken as its main protein ingredient. After ruling out all physical problems, with the exclusion of allergy testing, which was not done at the time (that I was aware of) I decided to make a radical change in Brody's intake and switch to a raw food diet. At the time, the only resource available to people that wanted to feed a raw diet was a book by Richard H. Pitcairn, DVM, PhD, and Susan Hubble Pitcairn titled *Dr. Pitcairn's Complete Guide to Natural Health*

for Dogs & Cats. Still in print, this book is a valuable tool, although there are now many books available on the subject.

Following the recipes in Dr. and Ms. Pitcairn's book, I transitioned Brody and Grace to a raw meat-based diet. That was about eighteen years ago, and I still feed a similar diet today with the exception of grains. Dr. Ian Billinghurst, an Australian veterinarian, revolutionized raw food diets around the world with his book, *Give Your Dog a Bone.* He says that grains cause all kinds of problems such as skeletal issues and cancer and are not normal in a canine diet.

When I changed Brody over to the new food, I was amazed at the change in his behavior. He was more puppy-like, more active and playful. Unfortunately, it did not solve his aggression problems—it had no impact on that—but Brody had more energy and spirit and his coat shone like it never had before. I was impressed and convinced that food could have a big influence on a dog's behavior. I have seen this in many of my clients' dogs as well.

If your dog has aggression issues, and especially if you have always fed him the same food, it can't hurt to try something new. Dogs can have allergies or food sensitivities that we don't know about, just like people can. While these often manifest themselves as skin or coat problems, behavioral problems can result as well. If you suspect a food allergy in your dog, consult with your veterinarian for testing. If you normally feed your dog chicken- and rice-based food, try beef or fish with potatoes instead. It is imperative that the treats you give your dog do not contain the ingredients you are trying to eliminate in the food or the experiment will backfire.

There is a plethora of foods and treats on the market today from which pet parents can choose. There are also many raw food companies that produce a commercial, prepared dog food for ease of use. I feed a combination of foods to my dogs: a commercially made raw food that contains ground meat, bone, organs, and vegetables; chicken backs that I get at a local butchering facility; and all of our leftovers or table scraps. I also throw in a few other items such as raw eggs, yogurt, and cottage cheese. With the exception of onions, grapes, and chocolate (chocolate can be fatal for dogs, even in small quantities), my pack eats everything we don't consume that we buy or cook.

In diets, variety is one of the most important elements. If you are trying a new diet, stick with a few main ingredients at first. If you notice a positive change in your dog, try the old food again and see if the old symptoms or behaviors come back.

Sometimes they will and sometimes they won't. It may be change the dog craves, and not necessarily a specific ingredient that is causing the problem. So you can often try a new food and then switch back to the old one without a change back in behavior. It's not the food itself that was causing the problem; it was feeding the same food all the time that was the problem. If you feed dry dog food, vary the type you give your dog. Switch every few bags from one kind to another, and do this for the life of your dog. If you decide to feed a raw food diet, it's just as important to vary what you feed. A single ingredient or even four of the same ingredients all the time is no healthier in raw food than in dry.

Dog to Dog Communication and Overstepping Boundaries

Miscommunications are not always a big deal. Sometimes it just means one dog does not play well with another. It may be a matter of them walking side by side or ignoring each other. But what happens when miscommunication becomes aggression? That's when the problems really arise. Aggression is when miscommunication goes too far. It is when one dog becomes hostile toward another. It may start with posturing, but often becomes fighting, albeit maybe one-sided.

An aggressive dog has lost its innate ability to work well with others of his own species. Or he may have been bred to be that way. Either way, an aggressive dog is no fun to own, especially if you live in a city or suburb where you encounter other dogs all the time. Aggression has many types and causes, and we are going to spend some time looking at those.

If you own an aggressive dog, you may read through these and see your dog in one or more of the categories. Types of aggression can overlap, and it is not uncommon for a dog to have more than one type, or sometimes show one behavior and at other times show a different behavior. Aggression can be situational and may not always be seen every time your dog sees another dog. It may only occur in your yard or in your car—or maybe only if there is food around. Whatever your situation, dog to dog aggression can be managed. With training, love, and patience you can teach your dog to behave in the presence of other dogs. Now let's look at types of aggression.

Types of Aggression
Dominance Aggression

The most common types of miscommunication or aggression are dominance-based and fear-based. Dominance aggression is seen in dogs who want to control other dogs and have supremacy over them. They usually have an upright body posture and attempt to tower over the other dog. Their hackles (the fur over the withers) stand up to make them look bigger. Their tails are erect and wagging stiffly. Their bodies are tense, they stand up on their toes, and they may be holding their breath. They may be showing their teeth and growling, or

Teeth displays are a sign of aggression. Although a bite does not always follow, the dog sure is thinking about it. *Credit: Sarah D. Todd*

they might have their mouths tightly closed. They make and maintain direct eye contact with the other dog.

If these dogs fight, they will often draw blood or cause injury of some kind. Their fights are scary and last several minutes, even if the other dog assumes a submissive posture. These altercations usually have to be broken up by a person in order to end the fight. Dogs can become dominance aggressive for a variety of reasons. The most common reason is genetics. Some dogs are just bred to be more dog-aggressive than others. Other reasons can include a traumatic interaction with another dog, or a dog being aggressed upon too many times by another dog. Sometimes the most submissive dogs can turn into the most dominant just from having the experience of being attacked so many times. They eventually want to "strike first" so as to avoid being hurt.

You can see dominance aggression (toward dogs) in any dog, but it is more commonly seen in the breeds I mentioned in Chapter 1, in which we discussed breed differences. An intact, male bully breed, for example, is much more likely to have dominance aggression than a neutered female retriever, although not always so.

I used to board a purebred Golden Retriever named Tara. Tara lived with me for many, many months. Initially Grace and Tara got along fine, not playing but not minding each other. But as time went on, they both wanted to be the dominant female in the house.

After Tara had been here for three or four months, she and Grace began to have fights, particularly on our hikes, but they spread into the house as well. At first the fights were mild, with neither dog being injured; but as their dislike for each other continued and they were forced to live together, the fights got nastier, with Grace finally being injured on the top of her head by Tara. I had to pour a bottle of Bitter Apple spray down Tara's throat to get the two of them to break it up. It was an awful, scary, unpleasant experience that I never predicted would happen. Their altercations had been mild up to this day. After that, Tara had to go live with an employee of mine because it was not safe to have her and Grace together.

Dominance aggression is also seen in guarding breeds that were genetically developed to work alone, in small, defined groups, or in pairs. An Akbash, a large white dog that was bred to guard livestock against predators, will not be friendly with unknown dogs. If exposed to certain dogs at a young age, pack members, or other guarding or herding dogs on its farm, it may be okay with them. But it will not take to new dogs on its property and may attempt to kill the intruder, as it was bred to do.

Unaltered male dogs will often have the worst cases of dominance aggression toward other dogs. That is not to say that all intact males will fight with others—they don't—but many of them do. Unfortunately, dominance aggression is not always helped by neutering if the dog is over two years of age because the

behavior has become learned. The dog has the habit of displaying aggression, and neutering may not have any impact on that. However, I *strongly recommend* neutering any dog with aggression issues because you do not want to breed a dog with serious behavior problems, and there is no other justifiable reason to keep a dog intact.

According to Dr. Anne K. G. Bazilwich, owner of the Grand Isle Veterinary Hospital in Grand Isle, Vermont, neutering is essential to stop the spread of undesirable traits and congenital diseases and disorders, including aggression. She said that although it is a controversial debate whether or not neutering will reduce or heighten the aggressive tendencies of dogs, there is no argument that aggression is heritable; therefore, neutering aggressive dogs is mandatory. Just as we do not want to breed dogs with known hip dysplasia, we absolutely do not want to breed dogs with known aggression.

Dominance aggression may be harder to manage than other types of aggression because of the tenacity displayed, but it is completely possible to teach this type of dog to behave in the presence of others. Brody, my German Shepherd/Golden Retriever mix, is a perfect example of overcoming dominance aggression.

As I wrote in the introduction, he became so aggressive with other dogs that I went from hiking him daily off leash with pleasure to having to keep him on a short leash at all times. This was a difficult and not fun change for us, since I feel that off-leash time is an essential part of dog ownership (if you can do it safely). I couldn't do it safely, so I had to stop taking Brody off leash in unfenced areas. I was very frustrated with this and desperately wanted to be able to continue hiking with him off leash.

I set to training Brody intensively in basic obedience. I taught him to heel and come away from other dogs when I encountered them. I had to have what I call "dog eyes"—I had to see the other dog before Brody so he wouldn't run up to it. If I was in an area where that was impossible, I kept Brody on leash. If I was in an open field or a trail where I could see down the path, I could successfully have him off leash. It made the majority of our walks fun for both of us.

Fear Aggression

Fear aggression is defined, as the name implies, by dogs who are scared of being in the presence of other dogs. It may come from genetics, a lack of socialization, or a breed predisposition to not being a pack-type animal. Genetics can play a role in any type of aggression, but fear-based aggression can often be seen in a puppy as young as only a few weeks old. Have you ever seen a litter of puppies and noticed that one shied away from the other pups? Or been to an animal shelter and seen the dog who cowered in the back of the pen? These dogs may have a genetic predisposition to be afraid of their own species. It really makes no sense from a survival viewpoint because as I've stated, dogs originally evolved to live in packs.

SIDEBARK

Jim and Topper

Topper was a purebred German Shepherd that belonged to a man named Jim. Topper and Jim lived in Burlington, Vermont, a small college town with houses built fairly close together. Jim and Topper encountered many dogs on their outings and bathroom breaks. When Topper got to be around two years of age, a common time for aggression to get worse because it's when dogs reach social maturity, he started becoming aggressive toward other dogs on his daily walks.

Jim came to see me to see how he could continue to own Topper when he could barely manage him on their walks down the sidewalk. I had Jim do desensitization training (see Chapter 3) and teach basic, but solid, obedience. By using the peanut butter container, at a distance at first, Jim was able to calm Topper when he came across other dogs. Jim also taught Topper to heel, sit, come, and look in the presence of all other dogs, and in doing so was able to walk Topper quietly down the street. When Topper came to see me the first time, he growled and lunged at other dogs. By the time Jim had spent six months training and desensitizing Topper to other dogs, they were able to enroll in an advanced obedience class.

If you own a young puppy that's scared of other dogs, get her into a puppy kindergarten class immediately. Contact your local humane society, your vet's office, and small, independently owned pet supply stores to find the name of a good local trainer. The window of opportunity to overcome this fear lies within the sixteen-week period when dogs can acclimate to new stimuli. Maybe your puppy was a singleton or maybe she got picked on in her litter. Regardless, *now* is the time to socialize her with other kind, gentle pups to help her get over her fears. Without intervention, fearful puppies will usually become aggressive dogs.

Fear aggression is more commonly caused by a lack of socialization than by breed differences. Once an owner gets a puppy home, he or she may only expose that puppy to a few other dogs. I hear many owners say they've socialized their pup to other puppies, and find out later that it's actually only been with three or four other dogs. That would be like having your three-year-old child only ever see three or four other kids. You would never consider that adequate socialization for a child, and it isn't adequate exposure for a puppy either. You must introduce your pup to numerous other puppies and dogs of all ages, shapes, and sizes for her to maintain the communication skills she learned in her litter. If you fail to continue to socialize your pup during the socialization period, she will lose the skills she learned in her litter and often become fearful of other dogs.

Fear aggression is displayed by a lowered, often submissive body posture. The dog will lower her front end and pull her head back into her shoulders. The fur all along the spine from the neck to the tail will often stand up. The ears

Deference behaviors are seen when one dog yields to the other, which usually means walking away. It's a good way to avoid an altercation.
Credit: Sarah D. Todd

Both dogs offer some appeasement as is seen in the raised paws. However, the dog on the left clearly defers to the advances of the Shepherd.
Credit: Sarah D. Todd

The hound mix in the front lowers her body to avoid any kind of fight with the Shepherd.
Credit: Sarah D. Todd

will automatically go back and the tail will tuck down low between the dog's back legs. The nose may lift up so the teeth are exposed if the dog is *really* afraid. The dog may even growl with a wrinkled nose. Eyes will be averted. In puppies, you may see submissive urination and they may roll onto their backs. Adult dogs will rarely roll over, being too scared to do so.

Fear-aggressive dogs look miserable when confronted with another dog. They will usually back away from the other dog if possible. If cornered, which the dog may feel just from being on leash, the dog may lunge forward and then retreat. This action may be repeated several times, often without making contact. If the dogs do connect, there are usually little to no injuries as the fearful dog is just trying to get the other dog to go away. Fearful dogs do not enjoy confrontation the way a dominance-aggressive dog seems to do. They don't like or want the challenge of coming face to face with another dog.

Territorial Aggression

Occurring primarily in a house, yard, or car, territorial aggression often contains some of the same components of dominance aggression. Interestingly, territorial aggression can also occur anywhere you regularly walk your dog. If you have a route you take every day with your dog for bathroom breaks, your dog will consider this *his* territory and he may become protective of it.

Almost all dogs show some amount of territorial aggression. Simply barking when there is a knock on the door or the doorbell rings is a display of this. The same thing is true if a dog walks by your house, yard, or car. Most dogs display mild to severe barking, and many dogs calm down once reassured by the owner. If taken to the extreme, the behavior can turn into aggression. Dogs that jump, lunge, snarl, or try to bite the dog approaching the house, yard, or car are said to be displaying territorial aggression. This is a prime example of communication taken to an extreme.

Most of us want our dogs to bark when a stranger approaches with a dog, but we want the dog to stop before it gets to the point of aggression. How confusing our world is to our dogs! How are they supposed to know when to stop? When is the barking enough? They often don't have a clue, and that's when you get aggression.

Guarding breeds are particularly prone to this type of aggression. Their instincts tell them any person or dog they don't know is an intruder and should not be allowed on the property. Their large, muscular frames pose quite an invincible front when a person tries to come into the house or another dog walks on the property. Fighting breeds can also be more likely to have territorial aggression than some of the more passive sight hounds, scent hounds, or gun dogs.

Luckily, some dogs have the perfect amount of aggression, like Tucker, my ten-year-old rescued Golden Retriever. My house is circled by a picket fence in which Tucker loves to hang out. If someone walks or bicycles down our dirt road with a dog, Tucker goes ballistic. He races the fence line, lunges, and barks. He shows his teeth and looks and sounds quite menacing. When I hear my dogs barking at the fence line, I immediately go outside and call them in so they are not a nuisance to other people. I don't really mind this, although sometimes he takes it to an extreme and it gets annoying. The good news is that when I go to the gate or allow someone to come into the house with her dog, Tucker is sweet as pie. He puts his ears back and wags his tail low. While Tucker is being territorially aggressive, he keeps it in check and does not carry through on the aggression. It's just not in his breed or his nature, his personal being, to be more aggressive.

Territorial aggression displays itself with much of the same body language as dominance aggression. The dog will exhibit forward body motion, stretching ahead of his front legs. His head will be held high and his hackles may come up. The tail will usually be high and stiff. Vocalizations will sound deep, loud, and throaty. Often the lips will be curled back and the dog will show his teeth. He will throw himself against the front door, car window, or fence. These dogs act like if they were to get through the barrier holding them back, they would *definitely* bite.

This type of aggression is moderately problematic, as it is contained to very specific circumstances and usually occurs when the dog is confined, except in the case of the dogs that are territorial on the street where you walk them on

The dog on the right gives all the signals of submission (lowered ears, head, and body) to the dominant dog on the left (raised head, ears, and tail, and hackles are up). *Credit: Sarah D. Todd*

a daily basis. Then you have to worry about any dog that may turn the corner and walk down the street toward you. Dealing with this kind of aggression will be discussed later.

Possessive Aggression

Toys, dog beds, furniture, and even humans can cause dogs to become aggressive. My Border Collie, Grace, had two kinds of possessive aggression. The first was that when she had a tennis ball she would growl at any dog that came near her. If she was without a ball, she was fine with the other dogs. But Grace was obsessed with her ball and did not want any other dog to get it. Also, if Grace was lying at my feet and another dog approached, she would often growl at the offending dog. If Grace was at a distance from me, she was fine with all dogs. Grace showed dog to dog aggression in only those situations. And I would be more apt to call it communication. She never attacked, she rarely did more than growl, but she just wanted the other dogs to know to stay away from me and to stay away from her ball.

Many dogs are very controlling of their toys. This is why at doggie playtime at dog schools or at the dog park, it is best if there are no toys. The dogs will focus on each other and not get wound up over toys. On hiking trails, with multiple dogs, I have seen problems arise simply over sticks. Usually the best response is to get the dog to drop the stick and to walk on.

If you live with more than one dog, you may see that one of your dogs dominates the other over dog beds or human resting places. Wyatt, my little terrier mix, sleeps under the covers snuggled up against my side at night. If another dog or a cat comes near the bed, Wyatt attacks the covers where the intruder is. Fortunately, the blankets prevent Wyatt from doing any damage, but it is not pleasant to have him doing this just the same. Many dogs become very protective of their own beds (toward humans, too) and will not allow other dogs to come near them when they are on their beds.

Possessive aggression is usually characterized by a growl as the initial behavior of choice. You will see body language in the form of dominance aggression if the dog is protecting a toy and is standing up. The display of body language may be less obvious if the dog is lying down, and you may have to look for more subtle signs such as tensing up, holding the breath, and again listening for the growl. A dog will sometimes charge away from his bed or toy, briefly go after the other dog, and then quickly return to whatever he is guarding. The aggressive display is usually ephemeral because the dog does not want to give up whatever he is defending.

Offering a large number of toys for a small number of dogs can help alleviate this problem. For example, if I am giving out chew hooves to my dogs, I will toss out a dozen or more for six dogs so they can each guard a few and all will be happy. Of course, this excludes Oscar, who must go in his crate to eat all raw bones or similar items. Sometimes crating one dog is the best choice if you want to play ball with a different dog or you want to give out tasty chew items in a multiple-dog household. Crates can be loved by dogs, as they are by Oscar. If you slowly train your dog to a crate, he or she will enjoy going into it. Crates are a wonderful management and training tool as well as a safe haven for your dog.

Food Aggression

Similar to possessive aggression but only seen with food items, this can be problematic in training class, on hikes with multiple dogs, at dog parks, or in multi-dog households. I recently worked with two people and their food-aggressive dogs. The first was a woman whose dog displayed food aggression whenever any people food or dog food was around.

She took her dog to work on a construction site, where several other employees also brought their dogs. When they had a break or lunch time, she had to put her black Lab, Jojo, in the truck or she would go after the other dogs. The dog was normally free to wander around the construction site safely, off leash, because of the isolated location of the site. But Jojo would launch after any dog in the group when the people pulled out their food. She was saying, "This is mine, and you'd better back off." At first I was concerned that training Jojo would be hard, because we use food to desensitize dogs. How could we do that if the food was making her aggressive? But as the behavior session proceeded and I evaluated Jojo with other dogs, I saw that she had some generalized dog to dog aggression, not solely food-aggressive dog to dog aggression. Fortunately, the desensitization worked with her.

The second case I handled was a couple with two newly adopted dogs. Bailey was a nine-month-old Lab/Pointer mix, and Daisy was an eight-year-old Airedale terrier mix. Both had been adopted from a New York shelter at the same time. Whenever the people pulled food out of the refrigerator, Bailey growled and postured at Daisy. They also could not feed the dogs in the same room. In the latter case, it's easy to feed the dogs separately and then pick up the empty bowls when the dogs are done eating. But the situation where the couple could not even make a salad without the dogs fighting was a bit more complicated to control. Again, we worked on desensitizing Bailey to the presence of food with training.

In my household, all my dogs act differently around their food bowls. Kobe will walk away from his bowl if another dog approaches and I have to "protect" his food until he is done. My other dogs are much more likely to guard their food and growl if another one approaches while they are eating. Oscar, the most aggressive of the pack, eats in a crate, and Pippit, the four-and-a-half-pound Papillion, eats so slowly that I feed her in a crate, too. A crate is a great management tool, and should be used if it will easily solve your aggression problem.

Body language will be similar to possessive aggression, although I have often seen dogs launch into much more serious fights over food than over other objects. Many people with multi-dog households do not have problems with food aggression, so if you are thinking about adding a second or third dog to your household, don't refrain from doing so because of the fear of aggression. And again, if it's just at the dog's meal time, it's fairly easy to control.

Predatory Aggression

Predatory aggression is often breed-specific. Some breeds of dogs, such as Siberian Huskies or Greyhounds, have a much higher prey drive than other breeds. Prey drive is what you see when your dog chases a squirrel in the park. Most dogs have some level of this drive. Few dogs will pass up the opportunity to run after a chipmunk or bird if given the chance. But in some dogs, the prey drive is so high that they will chase down and hurt or kill another dog.

Prey drive may also surface in a dog when it hears another dog make a high-pitched bark or howl, essentially a dog's form of screaming. I was walking with my dogs one day, and my neighbor's little Jack Russell terrier was out. He started screaming with an awful, high-pitched noise because he was afraid of my approaching dogs. My Golden Retriever, of all dogs, went into prey mode and chased down the Jack Russell. I was afraid Tucker, the Golden, would hurt the Jack had I not intervened. Any screeching noise made by a dog, particularly a young or small dog, can set off the prey drive of another dog.

Prey-drive aggression is rarely seen if the non-aggressive dog is stationary, unless it's screaming, which doesn't happen often except in particular dogs. Normally, the non-aggressive dog must be moving in order for the aggression to be seen. He doesn't necessarily have to be running, but some movement is usually involved. And screaming dogs are usually trying to run away from the other dog, even if they don't know the other dog is aggressive.

Body language in prey-drive aggression can be harder to see, because motion is involved. But normally the aggressive dog will have his hackles up and his tail out or up, and he'll be moving as fast as he can go. If your prey-drive aggressive dog is on a leash and can't run, you are likely to see the same body language as you see in a dominance-aggressive dog.

Maternal Aggression

This hormonally produced behavior can occur during a real pregnancy, a false pregnancy, or while the female dog has puppies. According to

Dr. Bruce Fogle in his book *The Dog's Mind*, maternal aggression is worse in females without pups. If a female is having a false pregnancy, she will begin guarding objects such as her bed or toys. Females that think they are pregnant when they are not will often protect these objects as though they were puppies.

Occurring in wolves as well, "pseudo-pregnancy" in dogs often causes mammary gland development and production of milk. According to the *UC Davis School of Veterinary Medicine Book of Dogs: A Complete Medical Reference Guide for Dogs and Puppies*, edited by Mordecai Siegal, it was thought that in the wild, wolves in false pregnancy would serve as nursemaids and help with the survival of the pack. Dogs in this state may show possessive aggression, but it is strictly caused by the hormones in the dog's body. You may find your intact female protecting toys or other objects she has decided are her "puppies" if she is having a false pregnancy. Fortunately, maternal aggression is short-lived, on average lasting one to three weeks (but it can last as long as regular pregnancy—averaging sixty-three days). Watch for it in intact females after a heat cycle, during gestation, and during lactation.

Maternal aggression can be quite fierce, with an attack coming without warning. If there is a warning, the dog will normally emit a low growl and stand close to her puppies (real or imagined). She may put herself between the puppies and the offending dog. The best treatment is separation from other dogs for the time the intact female is showing this behavior. As it is short-lived, you will not have to deal with it once the female dog is over the pregnancy and lactation or false pregnancy. Consult with your veterinarian if you have questions or concerns about real or false pregnancies.

Herding-Drive Aggression

This is a big-time miscommunication in action. Herding-drive aggression is really one dog (the herder) trying to display his normal doggie behavior, which is then misunderstood by the non-herding dog. Having owned several Border Collies and done Border Collie rescue for many years, I have seen a great deal of this type of aggression.

What happens is that the herding dog runs and circles the other dog or dogs. The non-herding dog does not want to be herded, and reacts either aggressively or in his own play style. The herding dog gets frustrated because the non-herder is not responding "properly." The non-herder gets fed up with the herder, and a fight ensues.

Most herding dogs are quite soft and sensitive, and if a fight does break out it will usually end quickly, although not always. You never know how long a fight will last, so many of them do need to be broken up. But I would be less concerned about this type of aggression than dominance aggression, in which the fights seem to be the worst.

Training a super-solid recall and a quick down are easy ways to counteract this type of

Herding can, but often does not, lead to aggression. This Border Collie spends all his time herding and not interacting with the other dogs. *Credit: Detlev Hundsdoerfer*

aggression. Because the dog is herding before the aggression begins, if you can call your dog out of the herding then you can interrupt any chance of aggression. The down side to this is that you may be constantly calling your herding dog, and she may not be able to play or run.

Purebred Dogs and Aggression

My Bulldog, Oscar, is a piece of work. While many Bulldog owners may argue with me, I believe he's typical of the breed. I don't mean to pick on bullies, but Bulldogs have it rough. Bulldogs are just one of many examples of purebred dogs that have issues because of their genetics. We, as a society, really need to look at what we have done to dogs with selective breeding. We have tried to fine-tune dogs' appearances so extensively that we have also severely affected their behavior.

Temple Grandin and Catherine Johnson, in their book *Animals in Translation*, say that:

Purebred dogs also suffer some of the negative emotional and behavioral effects of single-trait selection. Often breeders will mate their dogs so as to exaggerate one distinctive trait in the breed, like the rough collie's long thin nose . . . anytime you selectively breed for one trait, eventually you end up with neurological problems. Once you start getting neurological problems, one of these problems is likely to be aggression, so it doesn't surprise me that purebreds have more aggression problems than mutts.

Bulldogs, with their trademark smashed-in faces and short tails, also cannot show proper dog communication. The shape of their bodies physically prevents them from showing proper body language. For example, they don't have tails to indicate levels of aggression or submission, nor proper lips, which also show emotions in dogs. Their teeth are usually showing, even when they are relaxed or sleeping. These traits can be seen in other breeds, either because they lack tails, like the Australian Shepherd or Springer Spaniel, or because they are brachycephalic (smashed face), like the Pekingese.

Traits like tight, curly tails can also cause miscommunication, because a tail in that position signals dominance, even when the dog may not be dominant at all. "People have unwittingly made life more difficult for dogs" says Lisa Barrett, agility judge and instructor. In addition to bad body structure, Barrett points to some of the haircuts dogs get that can make it look to other dogs like their hackles are up all the time. This can be seen in the show cuts of Poodles and Portuguese Water dogs, for example.

Chapter 5  The Dog Park Dog

Dog park dogs are dogs that are friendly and comfortable with most or all dogs. Most of these dogs want to play and socialize with others, and that's when they are the happiest. These are the dogs you see romping and frolicking with others at the park or in your own yard. Dog park dogs are some of the easiest to own, and if you have one, the work ahead of you is really just to teach your dog some basic manners so you can have control of him in the presence of others (so he's not obnoxious when he meets up with dogs). Friendly dogs are easy to take out on the sidewalk, downtown, or on a hiking trail. Refer to Chapter 3, and teach some basic obedience so you can control your dog when he meets up with others.

Finding a Dog Park Dog

Dog park dogs come in all shapes and sizes. Spirited and dog-aggressive dogs do, too, but if you're specifically looking for a dog park dog, there are some breeds to consider more readily than others.

While you must take many things into consideration before getting a dog, such as size, coat length, exercise requirements, and activity level, wanting it to be good with others of its species may be high on your list. If so, get a good breed book, such as Dr. Bruce Fogle's *The New Encyclopedia of the Dog* or Desmond Morris's *Dogs*, and look at what the breed's original purpose was. Refer to Chapter 2 of this book to get an idea of whether the breed you want is likely to be good with other dogs. Then you also need to socialize, socialize, socialize your pup with others. (Hopefully by now you realize how important this step is!)

If you are adopting an older dog, be sure to observe him with other dogs before you decide to adopt him. You can have the shelter or rescue personnel do this dog to dog observation before you get the dog to determine if he's good with others or not. If you already own one or more dogs, insist on a meeting of all the dogs before you adopt or purchase the new one. Adopting an older dog is an *excellent* way of knowing the adult disposition and temperament of the dog. Even if you get a puppy and socialize him, you can't guarantee his adult personality. If you want a guarantee, adopt an older puppy (older than eight months) or an adult (older than fifteen months). Then you can know for sure what the dog will be like with other dogs (and save a life!).

The Chemistry of Dog Relationships

Lillie Goodrich, co-owner and founder of Sweet Border Collie Rescue at Glen Highland Farm in Morris, New York, says, "As humans we could impulsively fall in love with many, many dogs but when adding one to an existing canine family, it's far better to insure the right chemistry ahead of time. Dogs are always honest when they meet other dogs. They will quickly tell you if there is an affinity between them."

She said that through signals such as sniffing and smelling, body posturing, and ulti-

These two dogs obviously have good chemistry between them. *Credit: Detlev Hundsdoerfer*

mately play signals, it's fairly easy to see whether or not a good connection will be made. At her farm, whenever a person who already has a dog wants to adopt one of her dogs, she has his or her dog meet three to five of her dogs before deciding which new dog the other dog likes best. Through this process of seeing the dogs "dance," the natural preferences of the potential adopter's own dog are obvious. This exercise is both eye-opening for the humans and invaluable for all of the dogs involved, said Lillie.

When I adopted Jigs from Glen Highland Farm in September of 2006, I took my smallest dog, Pippit the Papillon, and my biggest dog, Kobe the Shiloh Shepherd, with me to meet him. I could have brought all the dogs, but I knew that with a sampling of dogs I would get an idea of how Jigs would behave with my pack. Because Pippit weighed only four and a half pounds, it was imperative that I introduce her to Jigs before I took Jigs home.

Even though a dog might be good with most dogs, you have to be careful when you own a four-and-a-half-pound Papillon. Pippit has excellent dog skills, but I needed to be sure Jigs did, too. The rescue had told me that Jigs had done well with the other Border Collies at Glen Highland Farm, but I wanted to be sure he would be good with other breeds, too.

It is interesting to watch two dogs of the same breed interact, because they will have a unique style of play. And herding breeds don't always get along with others, as I said in the first chapter. This is true of many breeds, and if you are adding a member to an existing pack, you really need to take breed into consideration.

If the dog you are thinking about adopting is your first dog, then you only need to consider

Tongue Flicking

The "Tongue Flick," as called by Brenda Aloff in Canine Body Language *(see Resources) is a sign of discomfort or concern. Watch your own dog for this type of communication.*

Two on one action causes the Border Collie in the middle to flick his tongue.
Credit: Detlev Hundsdoerfer

While both dogs show tongue flicks, they have very different body language. The dog on the left has "whale eye" (whites of her eyes showing) as she expresses dominance of the Golden.
Credit: Sarah D. Todd

The terrier mix tongue flicks even as the Bulldog turns away in submission. Both dogs are mildly uncomfortable. *Credit: Sarah D. Todd*

The Rotti puppy flicks her tongue while showing submission as she plays.
Credit: Detlev Hundsdoerfer

whether you are looking for a dog park dog: Do you want your dog to be good with all the other dogs it meets? Is your dog going to be interacting with a lot of other dogs? Do you live in a neighborhood with lots of pets, or do you live in an isolated country home where other dogs are not an issue? Are you planning to travel a lot with your dog? Do you want to participate in dog sports where your dog will be required to be around other dogs all the time?

NOTE When considering buying a new dog, you must think about the next twelve to fifteen years of your life and try to imagine what you will want and need.

If you want a dog park dog, get a friendly, outgoing dog that was bred to work with other dogs. Don't get a guard dog or fighting dog. Get something that will have a predisposition to be good with others. If you already own a dog that isn't a dog park dog, and you wanted it to be one, you may have to get over your dream and accept what you have. Some dogs will never be dog park dogs, while some can be trained to be one. Sometimes you have to accept limitations and know that your dog can't be with others. You'll need to manage your dog accordingly in this situation (see Chapter 3).

When Having a Dog Park Dog Isn't a Walk in the Park

One of the problems I see with dog-friendly dogs is that they sometimes lack some of the proper behavior seen in mature dogs. Some

---

SIDEBARK

Murray and Lucy

Murray is a three-year-old neutered chocolate Lab that came to see me with his owner, Lucy. Lucy, a woman very active in dog sports, had intentionally gotten a dog she expected would be good with other dogs. Murray seemed to fit the bill. He was great with other dogs, absolutely loving the dog park and playing around whenever he could.

The problem was that Murray had been having issues at his dog agility club and at agility trials. Other dogs had reacted aggressively when he ran happily into their space, on several different occasions. None of these encounters had been serious, but all of them had been scary to Murray—and especially to Lucy.

Lucy came to me to see if there was something she was doing that was causing the problem, or if there were things she could do differently to help matters. I evaluated Murray with several of my dogs. In consults, I often safely expose my dogs to my clients' dogs to observe and evaluate behavior. None of my dogs have ever been hurt doing this because all introductions start on leash and the dogs are kept a distance from each other unless I am sure the dogs will be good together.

First I brought in Wyatt, my eight-year-old, neutered male Cairn terrier mix. Wyatt and I stopped about eight feet away from Murray and watched his reaction. Murray was all wiggles, straining at the end of his leash as he tried to get to Wyatt. (Because Wyatt is

continued on next page

Murray and Lucy (continued)

small and blind due to progressive retinal atrophy, I don't let him go face to face with strange dogs very often unless I have evaluated them with my other dogs and know them to be safe.) That meeting, lasting about sixty seconds, went all right, so I removed Wyatt and next took Kobe, my Shiloh Shepherd, in to meet Murray.

Kobe is a dominant male, without aggression, but with a presence that says: *Don't mess with me.* Funny thing about Kobe though, if a dog is aggressive toward him, he almost always turns tail and runs the other way. Sometimes in these routine introductions, however, Kobe will stand tall and even bark at the other dog.

As soon as Murray saw Kobe he went ballistic trying to get to Kobe. Murray showed no adult dog behavior. He was acting like a puppy, just like he acted with Wyatt. Last, I brought in Jigs, who plays all the time with the dogs to whom I introduce him. I let Jigs and Murray meet and watched as Murray immediately tackled Jigs with happiness and excitement. Murray showed few greeting behaviors or submissive gestures to Jigs—he simply assaulted him with love.

That's where the problem was. Most dogs don't see this type of behavior as "love," they see it as an insult to their personal space. Jigs thought Murray came on way too strong with his buoyancy and was offended by this behavior. Murray was not aggressive in any way, but his overexcitement was probably too much for most dogs.

Murray would make direct eye contact with and barrel over all dogs he met. His behavior offended some dogs—like the ones who attacked him at agility events—and while he was never aggressive, he was very offensive. Ultimately, Jigs *did* play with Murray and I gave several suggestions to Murray's owner. These consisted of teaching Murray a fantastic "Look" response, so that when Murray saw new dogs Lucy could get Murray to look at her instead of looking straight at the other dog. I also suggested that Lucy train Murray in basic obedience to increase her control of him in order to get all-around better behavior. These days, Murray has much more success when competing at agility trials and attending doggie events. He pays close attention to Lucy and does not get into trouble with other dogs.

friendly dogs are overly gregarious and don't know any boundaries. It is normal for dogs to have a space around themselves that they want respected, and the dog park dogs are usually the ones that invade this space. A lot of Lab owners, for example, come to me and say their dogs are always getting beat up by others. This is because these exuberant Labs often display puppy behavior when they are adults. These goofy breeds think everyone will love them, and they don't know when to back off, or when to keep their distance to start with! They tend to get right in the faces of other dogs and can cause a great deal of upset with a dog that wants his boundaries respected. It's the overly friendly dogs that often have the most problems with the spirited or dog-aggressive dog, because they don't know to keep their distance. This is why it is so important to keep your dog on leash until you know who and what other dogs may be around. Then you can do a controlled, leashed introduction.

Dog park dogs do tend to be wiggly and excited to see other dogs. If they meet up with another dog like themselves, they are usually fine. Their body language is normally relaxed to alert, with their tails parallel to the ground and their ears relaxed or forward. They breathe rapidly and move around a lot. As you will see in later chapters, stiffness is a sign that a dog is having negative issues with the other dog. But please know that "even the good communicators sometimes have a tussle, and it can make a lot of noise and can be really scary, but they work it out," says Lisa Barrett, dog agility judge, agility instructor, and former vice president of the Humane Society of Chittenden County. Sometimes there is even a puncture wound, but it's not life-threatening—more like a scraped elbow on the playground. All dogs have "arguments" sometimes, and it doesn't need to be cause for alarm or concern. As long as the dogs shake it off and resume playing, you don't need to worry about minor spats.

One of the biggest worries to a dog park dog owner is encountering the dog-aggressive dog. In Vermont, people hike all the time with their dogs off leash. My clients who have dog-

The small dog turns away as the Shepherd towers over him. *Credit: Sarah D. Todd*

However, the Shepherd refuses to back off and the small dog gets aggressive. *Credit: Sarah D. Todd*

aggressive dogs always tell me of hiking with their dogs on leash and encountering off-leash dogs. The owner of the off-leash dog will yell ahead that their dog is friendly and the owner of the dog-aggressive dog will yell back that their dog isn't friendly. You can only imagine what kind of stress this situation can cause.

So, even if you own a dog park dog it's best to be respectful of all dog owners and keep your dog on leash unless or until you have complete off-leash control of your dog. This is not impossible; it just takes a lot of hard work (see Chapter

3). If you do come across an aggressive dog, try to body-block your dog with your legs. Keep your dog close to you and pivot as best you can to keep the dogs apart.

The Importance of a Leash

If the meeting is absolutely inevitable, then the *only* safe thing you can do is to give your dog some slack in the leash and let her defend herself. Obviously, this is very scary but if you tighten up on your leash you actually make your dog defenseless. This is no good. Instead, give your dog slack in the leash, or better yet drop your leash if it's safe to do so, and let your dog protect herself. The exception to this is if you own a dog small enough to pick up. If this is the case, quickly pick her up and turn your back to the aggressive dog. Hope that the owner of the aggressive dog appears quickly and gains control of his or her dog. Once the encounter is over, remember to *avoid* reassuring your dog.

Remember, reassurance equals praise and will make your dog's behavior worse. Assess for injuries and then go on your way if there are none. Fortunately, most dog fights do not result in injury, and hopefully this will be the case if your dog comes across an aggressive dog.

Owning a dog park dog can be fun and rewarding. It allows you lots of options with your dog. You can take her swimming, hiking, or down the sidewalk without worry. Just remember to keep control of your dog for the benefit of all dog owners. Enjoy!

Chapter 6 The Spirited Dog

Sam Punchar, executive director of The Dog School, designed and implemented our Spirited Dog class at the training center. Sam describes spirited dogs as "dogs that can be tense or uneasy with other dogs for reasons including fear, dominance, or a lack of exposure. Spirited dogs are often mainly all talk and rarely, if ever, cause injury beyond a simple puncture wound. These dogs tend not to be welcomed at dog parks or training classes, but with management and training they *do* have the potential to relearn the proper dog skills needed to communicate."

No one chooses to own a dog with problems, but if you have a dog who has issues, it's preferable to have a spirited dog as opposed to a dog-aggressive dog. You need to evaluate your dog fairly to ascertain which type of dog you

have, and then learn how to deal with her and train her accordingly. The biggest difference between the two types of dogs is that the spirited dog usually gets along well with others—not *sometimes* but *usually*. Not *always*, or he'd be considered a dog park dog.

Spirited Dogs Can Be Unpredictable

Basically, the spirited dog falls in between the two extremes. As with the dog-aggressive dog, you need to choose the times you want to introduce your dog to other dogs. You can do so frequently with the right introductions. By understanding dog body language (refer to pictures throughout the book), you will know if your dog is going to get along with the other dog or not.

NOTE It is wise to err on the side of caution, and if you are worried during an introduction, abandon it. Your spirited dog will find another playmate another time.

In some ways, the spirited dog is hardest to own. If your dog were aggressive with all or most dogs, you would know to keep her away from them. And if your dog were friendly with all dogs, you would never need to worry about playing together. But with the spirited dog, you need to treat each introduction as a potential for a problem, and hope one doesn't arise. Punchar says, "It is the responsibility of the owner of the spirited dog to keep their own dog as well as everyone else's dogs safe. That is why it is so crucial to learn what triggers your dog. Once you know what type of dog sets your dog off, you can practice obedience and desensitization exercises to help deal with the issues. It is important to understand that the spirited dog is unpredictable and should be monitored closely in all encounters. If you are unsure of how your

The teeth on the Golden tell the Border Collie mix to turn away and he does. *Credit: Sarah D. Todd*

dog will react it is best to assume the worst and be ready and prepared."

If an altercation does occur, try to get your dog out of there as quickly as possible. Pull your dog away and body block the other dog from making contact with your dog. As described in the previous chapter, if the encounter is inevitable and nothing you can do will prevent the dogs from making contact, then slacken your leash and let your dog defend himself. Then when there are two people present, try to safely separate the dogs.

First Time Fenced-In Meetings

There are several ways to introduce your spirited dog to another dog. If you have any question about whether there is going to be a problem, then a controlled introduction is best. The ideal way to do this, as with a dog-aggressive dog, is with a fence between the dogs. You can never go wrong with that type of introduction. If you have one dog in a fenced yard and the other dog on the outside of the fence, you can quickly determine whether the dogs are going to get along. The dog on the outside of the fence must be allowed a *loose* leash, as much as possible. A tight leash can cause problems and will not allow your dog to communicate freely with the fenced dog.

If your dog is good off leash, have her outside the fence off leash. If there is a fence between the dogs, you never have to worry about them fighting. If a fenced meeting is possible, do no intervention, say nothing, don't pet the dogs—

just let them be together and see what they say to each other. If they appear fine, then you can put them into the fenced yard together.

A spirited dog will have the majority of problems upon introduction. If your dog is fine with the fenced meeting and shows no signs of aggression, then it's probably safe to put the dogs in the yard together to play. If there are problems upon introduction, such as snarling or attacking the fence, you might not want to put these two dogs together. Usually if you try it once and the dogs don't do well together, then a second meeting probably won't make a difference with this specific dog. A different dog is likely to get a new reaction. Dogs that have issues often don't like a certain type of dog and are concerned with size or color or gender. Your spirited dog will probably be fine with dogs of one gender or the other, or of a certain shape or size. As I say in the dog-aggressive dog chapter, you need to choose your battles. If this was just a happenstance meeting and the dogs don't have to like each other, and the introduction went poorly, you might want to walk away at this point. If, on the other hand, you really need these dogs to get along, let the dogs interact with the fence between them and allow them to say whatever they want to say for several minutes.

Wait and see if they can work it out with the fence between them. Often, after a few minutes, the dogs will settle down and get along—they might not play, but they might relax around each other. If they don't settle down, reevaluate whether you must have these dogs together. Spirited dogs don't usually change from aggressive to tolerant. They usually pick the dogs they like, and if they don't like a certain dog it usually stays that way. You may find that you simply cannot have your dog play with the dog, as you hoped. However, this is not always the case.

My dog Oscar is an odd example of a spirited dog. Because of the dog boarding business I run out of my home, Oscar is forced to get along with new dogs all the time. While Oscar would do best in a home with no other dogs, or with a dog that was clearly much more submissive than he is, he lives in my crazy household and has to function with the other new dogs. (Since being on Fluozetine—generic Prozac—he hasn't fought with any boarding dogs.)

I have a "dog room" where many of the boarding dogs stay, but most of the dogs get time in the house and some of the dogs stay in the house all the time. Recently, Phelix, an eleven-month-old Cavalier King Charles Spaniel, came to board for six weeks. Since Phelix is too small for the dog room, he stays in the house full time.

I have a routine with Oscar that seems to work and you could certainly try this with your spirited dog as well. When a new dog is coming, I put Oscar in his crate. Oscar loves his crate because great things happen there: he gets Kong toys, breakfast, dinner, and other yummy goodies when he's inside. If your dog isn't crate trained, you might need to train him before bringing new dogs into your house. The crate allows for "time-outs," as well as a safe place to put your dog if he starts acting out. So, when a new dog like Phelix comes to the house, I crate Oscar. He sits in his crate in the dining room and waits for the new dog to come near him.

Phelix is a perfect example of what happens when new dogs come to the house. When Phelix came, he started running around, sniffing all the new things and checking out the other five dogs in the house. When Phelix walked by Oscar's crate, Oscar growled loudly. Oscar didn't lunge at the crate door, but his hackles all came up and he sounded quite loud and fierce. I ignored Oscar's growling, and when he became quiet, I praised him. Every time Phelix approached Oscar's crate, Oscar growled. I continued to ignore Oscar. This continued for about three hours, and then Oscar finally settled down.

After several hours of growling (and me not paying attention to him), Oscar will accept the new dog and then I can let him out of his crate. With Phelix, I had Oscar in his crate for the required three hours and then I let him out. I watched him closely, ready to intervene if need be. But I have done this many times and I know how Oscar will behave. When I let him out of his crate, he simply ignored Phelix. Oscar walked around on his tippy toes, ready for a fight, but I know from so many experiences that he would tolerate Phelix's presence.

Finding Outside Assistance

Sometimes two dogs in the same household vie for dominance. This can be a frustrating and sometimes unsolvable problem. If you have two dogs in the house that constantly fight with each other, definitely seek the help of a professional trainer who can help you evaluate whether or not the two dogs can live together. Check with your local humane society, your veterinarian's office, and your local pet supply store to get names of good trainers.

In my household, it would be better if Oscar and Wyatt didn't live together, but my husband is unwilling to re-home his Bulldog and I am unwilling to re-home Wyatt. After several fights, including a few when Wyatt needed stitches, we put both dogs on Fluoxetine. This has helped tremendously, and while the dogs have spats sometimes, they never fight like they used to and Wyatt (who weighs thirteen pounds to Oscar's fifty-nine pounds) has thankfully not been injured again. Medication doesn't always work, and I have had some clients whose two dogs absolutely could not learn to get along, even with medication, and one of the dogs had to be re-homed.

Coming Up With Your Own Routine

I found a routine with Oscar that works and you, too, may find that you can have a pattern that works for your spirited dog. The most important thing to do is to set up a safe introduction. If a fenced yard is not available to you, the next best thing is to put up a baby gate in a house and then let the dogs meet with the gate between them. You might want to keep the dogs' leashes attached in case the gate comes down, but don't pull back on the leash.

When people see two dogs start to fight, automatically the first thing they want to do is stop it. But if the dogs can't hurt each other, it's usually best to let them work it out for a bit and see what happens. As much as I wish we could, you can't make two dogs like each other. You can teach your dog to behave in the presence of other dogs (see Chapter 3) but you cannot teach him to play with or enjoy the company of another dog.

Over time, the dogs will eventually acclimate to each other, and usually this happens pretty quickly. Giving it three or four hours, like I do with Oscar, is not the norm, but you should be open to trying anything that's safe. If your dog is crate trained, you can certainly use the crate as a protected way to introduce your dog to another. The crate must be a happy place for your dog; if it's not, or if your dog isn't crate trained, please crate train him before you use this method. If the uncrated dog does not want to go near the crate, you can use a leash to guide the loose dog over to the crate. The goal is always to have the dogs meet safely.

Leashed Introductions

If a fence, a gate, or a crate is not an option, the next best thing is to have the dogs meet on leash. While I hate to see a taut leash because it can cause two dogs to be aggressive due to the frustration of the restraint, if you don't have another option, leashes will work.

The best way to do leashed introductions is to have the two dogs at a distance from each other. There is no set amount of space this should be, but err on the side of more distance, say at least 60 or 70 feet, rather than less. Just letting the dogs see each other at a distance—perhaps a block apart or across a parking lot—might be a good place to start.

Observe how your dog reacts to the sight of the new dog. Do not talk to your dog, ask your dog for a certain behavior, or interfere in any way. Let the dogs talk without your interacting with the dog at all. If all is good, and there are no negative signs (see photos throughout the book), move the dogs closer to each other. If your dog is reactive, wait a bit. If your dog calms down, give him a tasty tidbit such as a small piece of chicken or steak and praise him verbally. Then move closer. As you approach the other dog, stay calm and continue to reward your dog with small treats—but only if your dog is calm. If the food seems to just be getting in the way, then it's okay not to use it.

Slowly move the dogs closer together. As the distance lessens, watch your dog for signs of discomfort. If all is good, keep moving the dogs together until they can greet and say hello. This may be one of those encounters when your dog is going to be fine, and then you can let the dogs be together and enjoy each other. If there is tension, one dog starts holding its breath, there is growling, or you notice other signs of aggression, you might need to turn and walk the other way. You have a spirited dog, and he is not going to get along with everyone. If it is essential that these two dogs get along, follow the instructions in Chapter 7. If it's a chosen encounter that can be avoided, walk away.

NOTE Remember, not all situations are going to go well. But keep in mind that some amount of behavioral display is okay. It's okay for your dog to set up a space around himself with which he feels comfortable. You need to watch for the more serious signs of aggression and try to decide if these two dogs can be together. With a spirited dog there will be times when you just can't have your dog with the other dog. You must accept this and move on.

Mounting

Once you have done several introductions, you will learn your dog's modus operandi (MO). You will know if your dog has a rough start and then is fine. Many spirited dogs are that way. Many just need to get through the first few minutes together and then they are fine. That is, unless the other dog mounts them.

Mounting is a normal behavior that both male and female dogs use to express dominance over each other. Many dogs like to mount others, and it is always a display of dominance unless it involves an intact male and female. Mounting often causes problems, although not always.

Tucker, my ten-year-old rescued Golden Retriever, is clearly the most dominant in my pack. He is a benign and judicious leader, and

if you didn't live with him you would never know he was the head of the doggy household. Lots of dogs like to mount Tucker in a mock display of dominance. It's a test and Tucker tolerates it. But if a dog were truly to challenge him, he would fight. Sometimes I intervene when dogs mount Tucker and sometimes I just ignore it. If I think a fight is about to ensue, I will definitely stop the mounting. In playtime in my obedience classes, we interrupt all mounting because it can lead to aggression and we need to keep things calm and mild at group playtime.

Mounting is an expression of dominance seen in all ages and all types of dog to dog communication. *Credit: Sarah D. Todd*

Few spirited dogs will tolerate mounting. It's as though they are not secure enough in themselves to withstand the challenge. Tucker knows he's more dominant and he doesn't need to fight. But a spirited dog has some level of insecurity which, when tested, will cause him to fight.

Dogs Have Insecurities, Too

Most spirited dogs do have some level of insecurity. They don't know where they stand in the world, and so they sometimes fight. Rarely alpha, they are what I call "wannabes" or betas. They want to be the top dog but they aren't. They are often the "party police," breaking up others when they play and never joining in themselves.

These dogs give mutual dirty looks and the dog on the left furthers her dominance by wrinkling her muzzle. *Credit: Sarah D. Todd*

Both dogs are threatening each other but they don't act out. Notice the appeasement gesture (raised paw) in the Border Collie. *Credit: Sarah D. Todd*

Penny

Penny, an eight-year-old, spayed, female Hound/Husky mix is a spirited dog that is clearly *not* into other dogs playing. She lives in a pack of seven and gets along fine with all her housemates, but when she meets new dogs, she comes on strong, with overstated body posture, tail raised, ears forward, and standing tall. She often needs controlled introductions.

Not the most dominant in her pack, she does play sometimes with the other dogs in her house. But if the other dogs in her house are playing without her, she barks, runs over, and body slams the dogs until they stop playing. The other dogs stop playing and often look sad or confused. Penny also steals toys away from other dogs, not necessarily because she wants them, but because she certainly doesn't want the other, less dominant, dog to have them. She would like to be the most dominant in her pack but she just isn't, because there are other, more dominant dogs in the house. If her owner wants the other dogs to be able to play, she has to put Penny in another room or Penny will stop the play session. Penny could never go to the dog park, not because she would necessarily fight with the other dogs, but because she would stop all the other dogs from playing.

Penny is just one type of spirited dog. She was well socialized, so no one knows for sure why she acts this way. The best thing to do to try to prevent your dog from becoming like this is to socialize her at an early age, and keep up on playtime with other dogs as your dog gets older. But some dogs will just grow up this way, and we will never know why.

Kobe

Kobe, my Shiloh Shepherd, is another spirited dog. They come in so many shapes and sizes that I'd venture to say more dogs tend to be spirited dogs than dog park dogs. Kobe's MO consists of issues upon greeting other dogs. He comes on very strong and dominant. Given the chance, he would try to bite almost any new dog he meets. If you met him, you would never suspect this behavior. Normally he is submissive. If a familiar dog threatens him in any way, he turns tail and runs. He is actually quite omega, but not upon greeting.

To control Kobe's greetings, I always put him on leash and approach the other dog slowly. I try to keep the leash slack if at all possible. The other thing I do, and this may seem mean, is to squirt Kobe, a few times, with water proactively. I know the water will grab his attention, and I've found that if I spray him *before* he makes contact with the other dog, he won't go after it. It may seem a little unkind, but it works. I know I'm going to have to spray him as soon as he makes contact with the new dog so it's easier if I spray him before they meet. I feel mean when I do this, it seems unfair, but I have conducted so many introductions with Kobe and new dogs that I know he will try to bite or tackle them otherwise. Once the greeting is over, Kobe never has issues with other dogs. He interacts and coexists with all the boarding dogs and does just fine. It's only upon greeting that I have to control him. Kobe is a classic example of a spirited dog.

Talking the Talk

I have given you many options for introducing your spirited dog with others. The goal is to always have success in the dogs' first encounter, and thus be able to put them together to play. As Sam Punchar said at the beginning of the chapter, spirited dogs are usually "all talk" and rarely injure another dog. So after they have met, it is usually safe to put the dogs in together and allow them to interact.

The more introductions and new playmates your spirited dog has, the better he will get at cooperating with others of his own species. Remember, all dogs (except singleton pups) developed some amount of social skills in their litter. By interacting in new play groups, your dog is regaining the skills he learned as a puppy. As he has more and more encounters, he should get better and better at playing. He will probably always choose his playmates carefully, not loving every dog he meets, but he will coexist peacefully with most of them. Again, repeated interactions are key.

The more new dogs your dog meets, the better he will become at both meeting and interacting with others. Seek out classes where the instructor has experience with spirited dogs, or where the dog training school has specific classes for them. If you cannot find a class that suits your dog, ask your dog-owning friends if they are willing to bring their dogs over to your house, or better yet, have the dogs meet at their house. It's true that neutral ground is best, but if it has to be one house or the other, you're better off at the other dog's house. That way your dog can't show possessive or territorial aggression. But if you are the only one with a fenced yard, then by all means, use your house.

The fenced yard is always the safest way to do introductions. But if you don't have access to a fenced yard, there are many other options available to you for greetings. Once you have done the greeting, let the dogs play. If your dog doesn't want to play, just being in the presence of the other dog will be helpful. Your dog may not want to interact much with the other dog, but there is always "dog talk" going on if the two dogs are awake and in the same room.

Repetition Reaps Rewards

People can get "vibes" from each other. They can communicate in a room without actually talking. You can usually tell if someone is in a good mood or a bad mood simply by picking up on body language. You can tell a lot about someone by the way she is sitting, holding her hands, or moving her head, or by the tone of her voice. This is all true for your dog, too. Even if your dog is not playing with the other dog, he's still learning something just from being in the presence of the other dog.

Imagine that there was something you were afraid of, say a flying bat, and I was trying to help you get over it. Just one exposure to a bat wouldn't do much to relieve your fear. But if I kept putting you in the presence of flying bats, you would slowly get used to them. It might take several repetitions, but eventually you

would get less and less scared of flying bats and become more comfortable with them in general. The same thing is true for your dog; the more he is exposed to the new dogs the more comfortable he will be with them. It may take numerous exposures, but eventually he *will* get more accustomed to the new dogs. (By the way, bats are the only creatures I am afraid of!)

The Seriousness of Injuries

At the beginning of the chapter I quoted Sam Punchar as saying that spirited dogs "rarely, if ever, cause injury beyond a simple puncture wound." And that sentence may have scared many of you. Chapter 2 covered how people react to dog to dog miscommunication. After having worked with dogs for so long, I feel that a small puncture wound is no worse then a skinned knee on the playground. I take small injuries with a grain of salt.

Now, many people may disagree, but a small, simple puncture wound is not the end of the world. Yes, even a tiny puncture wound can become infected; you're right. And it is important to check with your vet if your dog gets punctured, because the wound may require treatment. But even so, this is a small injury compared to what I have (unfortunately) seen dog-aggressive dogs do.

At The Dog School, we schedule our Dog to Dog Communication class, the class for dogs with serious aggression issues with other dogs, to start a week or two after the Spirited Dog class starts. That way, if a dog is too aggressive for the Spirited Dog class, it can go right into the Dog to Dog Communication class. Sam teaches the Spirited Dog class and evaluates all the dogs on the first night of class. She determines in which class a dog belongs by watching its level of aggression. If it's mildly aggressive and does okay meeting most of the other dogs, it's in her class. If it's overly aggressive with one dog or somewhat aggressive with all the other dogs, then it takes my class.

It is important to remember that most people want all dogs to be happy all the time and never display any miscommunication. That is as unrealistic as expecting a person to always be in a good mood. It's just not normal for dogs always to want to play and always to love each and every dog they meet. If you've got one of those, that's great, but most dogs are not happy all the time with other dogs.

NOTE Remember, try to control your dog's greetings, where the most problems are likely to occur and then, if all goes well, allow your dog to play or hang out as long and as repetitively as possible.

Chapter 7   **The Dog-Aggressive Dog**

So you have an aggressive dog. Hopefully by now you have come to realize it's not the end of the world. It's not what you had hoped for, but there it is. I have been there. I am still there with the dogs I live with now.

I define a dog-aggressive dog as any dog that always or often fights with another dog. Even if there are no injuries, there is usually a lot of noise and engagement. It's scary and not fun to watch two dogs fight, or one dog attack another. Sometimes these fights can lead to injuries, sometimes not, but they are normally loud and distressing.

Dog to Human Aggression

It's not easy to own a dog-aggressive dog, but take relief in knowing that dog to dog aggression does not equal or lead to dog to human aggression. By the same token, aggression toward humans will not necessarily lead to dog to dog aggression. Your dog could have both dog to dog *and* dog to human aggression, and in that case, seek the help of a qualified professional trainer to guide and assist you. For the most part, however, you don't need to worry that one type of aggression will lead to the other.

Kelley Bollen, MS, dog behaviorist and trainer from Massachusetts, said that in her experience, dogs that are aggressive to other dogs are not more likely to develop similar aggression problems toward humans and vice versa. Dog to dog issues usually stem from either a lack of socialization to other dogs or a bad experience with another dog. Although aggression toward humans can stem from the same factors—a lack of socialization or a bad

Signs to Watch for in a Dog-Aggressive Dog

In this series of photos, Trout becomes increasingly aggressive while in the presence of another dog. Pay close attention to the shift in her ears, the look in her eyes, and the changes in her muzzle.

All photos credit: Sarah D. Todd

experience—these two contributing factors are typically species specific.

She added that any dog that wasn't socialized well with other dogs may have had plenty of socialization with humans. There are numerous contributing factors leading to aggression, such as a tendency to guard resources. In the case of canids, possession aggression toward members of your own species is very normal behavior. A dog who guards possessions from other dogs may be perfectly fine relinquishing the same items to humans. "Of course there are dogs who exhibit aggression to both dogs and humans, but one does not necessarily transfer to the other," she concluded.

Control and Play Are Two Different Things

Remember, you are not the cause of your dog's aggression, and there is hope. The hope is that you *can* teach your dog to behave in the presence of other dogs. This is not the same as playing with other dogs; control and play are very different things. Many, if not most, dog-aggressive dogs cannot play with others. If your dog is aggressive for any of the reasons discussed in Chapter 4, then you may need to follow the desensitization exercises in Chapter 3 to gain the control you need in the presence of other dogs. If you feel that your dog may be tolerant of some other dogs but aggressive toward others, be sure to use caution at every introduction.

First, choose your battles. If you have a friend coming over for the evening, ask her to leave her dog at home. It's not worth the work it would take to get the dogs comfortable with each other. If, on the other hand, you just met the love of your life and he or she has a dog, it may now be imperative that the dogs get along. Below are a few ways to determine whether the dogs can ever be together.

Use a Chain Link Fence

The safest and easiest way to introduce two dogs that might have problems (even if it's just one dog that seems to have the problem) is to use a chain link (or similar but not solid) fence. Have one dog on each side of the fence. If possible, it's best to have both dogs off leash. If you can only have one dog (the dog inside the fence) off leash, then so be it. For the dog that is leashed, remember to keep your leash as *loose* as possible. This is extremely important. Tight leashes can cause barrier frustration as well as transmit owner stress to the dog. If you must have your dog on leash for safety reasons, move

Using a chain link fence as a barrier between two dogs that are meeting for the first time is a great safety precaution. *Credit: Detlev Hundsdoerfer*

toward the other dog (that's on the other side of the fence). There is zero risk of injury if there is a fence between your dog and the other dog, so don't worry.

Let the two dogs "talk" and say whatever they want to say. Sometimes, when humans don't interfere, dogs will work out what they want to say to each other and then be fine together. With the fence between them, nothing bad can happen. Let the two dogs talk all they want to each other. If the non-aggressive dog is scared and wants to run away, then don't force it to make contact with the aggressive dog. If the less aggressive dog wants to check out the more aggressive dog, that's great. Let them say their piece with the fence between them. Even if they are trying to attack each other, which is likely to happen at the beginning of any dog-aggressive introduction, let them be without your interference. By referring to the pictures throughout the book, you can read your dog to see what she is saying to the other dog. It will be pretty obvious if your dog is too aggressive to put the dogs inside the fenced yard together. If the dog-aggressive dog is going ballistic, then don't put them in together.

If, on the other hand, the aggressive dog is able to de-escalate and begins to show temperate or even play behavior, you might be able to put the dogs together. To do this, have a leash on each dog. Put them in the fenced yard together and let them drag their leashes on the ground. The actual leash won't cause the problem, but the nervous, stressed-out owner at the end of the leash—who is tightening it like mad—could.

Dragging Leashes

Once you have introduced the two dogs with the fence between them as a precautionary measure—and you have decided they are going to be civil toward each other—it's time to try this next step. Allow both dogs to drag their leashes—meaning to walk around with the leash dangling but no one holding onto it. Let them say hello to each other and sniff and posture. If all is still going well (keep breathing), simply continue to let the dogs get to know each other.

If a fight suddenly breaks out, you have two choices. The first is to let the dogs work it out on their own, while you stand back and observe, saying and doing nothing. If ultimately you must have these dogs like each other, this may be the only choice you have. It may be difficult to watch, but you just have to let them have at it.

NOTE Remember that you cannot force two dogs to like each other. We can make them behave in each other's presence, but we can't make them play or get along amicably without trying to let them work it out together. This can be a dangerous step to take, so do not take it lightly. You may try to let them work it out, and you may be rushing one dog to the vet's office in thirty seconds. Or you may break up the fight after any amount of time by pulling them apart with the leashes. I usually let the dogs interact on their own for about one minute unless the fight looks bad—fur flying, teeth gnashing, really going after each other.

There is no way to know for sure if a fight will break out. Hopefully by introducing the two dogs to each other with the fence between them first, you will know if they are going to fight. And if you do put them together—leashes dragging— and a fight ensues, you can break them up either immediately or at some point during the fight, usually after thirty to sixty seconds. To do this, use the leashes to safely pull the dogs apart. Warning: Do *not* reach in between the fighting dogs with your hands. If you do, you will most likely get bitten. I tell all my employees the fastest way to get bitten is by attempting to break up a dog fight. I have seen many horrible-looking fights where two dogs act like they are going to kill each other and, unable to break them up, I just watch and wait until they are over it. In the end, there are usually no injuries. I don't enjoy seeing fights, but with the number of dogs I have together at various times it is inevitable.

When a Muzzle Helps

An alternative to just letting the two dogs meet together inside the fence is to muzzle (with a basket-type muzzle) the aggressive dog or dogs. This allows for all kinds of safe contact without the risk of injury. You might still have a fight, but it's the teeth that do the most damage, and with the muzzle on you won't have any bites or tears. If you do this without muzzles then you

are taking a big risk. I often use muzzles if I have had time to meet with clients ahead of time and have asked them to muzzle train their dogs. Ideally, if I know a dog is aggressive, I would always use a muzzle for introductions if I could not have a fence between the dogs.

If you put two muzzled dogs together and a fight ensues, simply grab their leashes to gain control again. Remember to never use a tight leash on your dog when you're introducing him to another dog. *Credit: Sarah D. Todd*

The ABCs of Muzzle Training

Muzzles can buy you a lot of freedom. They can make the difference between a dog you can take out in public and one you cannot. This may be more useful with dog to human aggression than dog to dog aggression, but in both cases the muzzle can give you liberty to take your dog out in public. I encourage the use of muzzles if you live in a congested area where you often encounter loose dogs. Also, it's best to use a muzzle if you want to take your dog-aggressive dog on hiking trails or to family picnics. Training your dog to wear the muzzle comfortably is fairly easy—as is training anything else—by using food, love, and plenty of patience.

Proper fitting muzzles help to prevent unwanted altercations between dog-aggressive dogs.
Credit: Sarah D. Todd

First get a properly fitting, basket-type muzzle. These are usually made of wire or plastic or are vinyl-coated and can be found at your local pet supply store or searching on the Internet. For the best fit, follow the manufacturer's guidelines. *Do not* use cloth muzzles. They are used by groomers and veterinarians for short periods of time. Since cloth muzzles can only be used for a few minutes at a time, you must use a basket muzzle if you are going to take your dog somewhere in the muzzle. In my dog to dog communication class all the dogs are required to wear basket muzzles when they interact with each other. The owners spend two to three weeks training their dogs to wear the muzzle and then the dog is not uncomfortable having it on.

To train your dog to wear the muzzle, start as you would with the head halter. Touch the muzzle to your dog's face and feed him a yummy treat. Repeat three or four times in a row. Then repeat a few times throughout the day.

Next, slip the muzzle over your dog's nose and feed some treats through the side of the muzzle. This is easiest if you have a long treat such as a cheese stick or a dog jerky treat. Feed, feed, feed while the muzzle is on your dog's face. Leave it on for a few seconds, maybe ten, feeding the whole time, and then take it off. Repeat this four times during the day.

The third day, put the muzzle on and strap it around your dog's neck. Make sure it's snug and can't come off. Leave it on for about fifteen or twenty seconds and feed treats the whole time. Then unbuckle it and take it off. Repeat four times during the day.

On day four, put the muzzle on your dog and feed him some treats for fifteen seconds. Then stop feeding and leave the muzzle on for another fifteen seconds while you pet your dog in his favorite spot. Then take off the muzzle. Repeat four times throughout the day.

Next, slowly increase the time your dog wears the muzzle by fifteen-second increments. Each session should be a bit longer than the previous one, so your dog is wearing the muzzle for two or three minutes after a week or so. Always feed treats during the first fifteen or twenty seconds the muzzle is on and feed a few treats before you take it off. Give your dog lots of loving attention when he is wearing the muzzle, and not after you take it off.

When your dog is successfully wearing the muzzle for two minutes, you can put it on when you are going for a walk. Put the muzzle on, feed treats, and then put on your dog's leash and go for a very short walk, maybe a two- or three-minute walk. Then go inside and take the muzzle off. Again, praise your dog and shower him with affection *while* the muzzle is on, not once it comes off.

Slowly increase the time the muzzle is on your dog until he wears it comfortably for thirty minutes or more, or however long you need it to be. Always try to do fun things with your dog when the muzzle is on. You don't want anything bad to happen while the muzzle is on, so make it fun and use lots of treats!

Dog-Aggressive Dogs May Bite

Sam Punchar, executive director of The Dog School, was hiking with Rusty, a Golden Retriever, and Petey, a Bernese Mountain Dog, when the two dogs started to become aggressive toward each other. Sam kept walking, hoping the small altercation would end, but the fighting actually began to get worse. Sam stopped and ran back to the two dogs, grabbing Rusty's collar because Rusty was winning the battle. As soon as Sam grabbed Rusty, Petey bit her hard on the wrist. The dogs finally stopped fighting, but Sam ended up with five puncture wounds and a fast trip to the emergency room. Meanwhile, neither dog ended up with a scratch.

It's Your Call

You have a few choices if you put the dogs together and they begin to fight. You can either let them work it out until they're over whatever caused the fight in the first place, let them try to work it out then eventually break it up, or intervene at the first sign of a fight. You really need to know your dog to help you make the best decision. For example, if your dog has caused serious injuries to another dog before, you may not want to let any fighting occur the next time you see your dog starting to act up.

Recently, I worked with a family with a pack of five dogs—two Pugs, a Lab mix, a Catahoula Leopard dog mix, and an Australian Shepherd. This is a sad story, as one of the Pugs died. The five dogs were owned by a couple that lived in a house with a tenant living in an apartment attached to the main part of the house. The dogs were home alone, but the tenant who lived in the apartment heard the whole thing and tried to rescue the Pug.

The dogs' family told me that the tenant had heard a horrible-sounding dog fight through the wall from the main part of the house into the apartment. She ran over to the main house and saw Sally, the Australian Shepherd, and Mala, the Catahoula mix, attacking one of the Pugs. The tenant was able to finally pull the larger dogs off the Pug, but it was too late. The Pug was rushed to the vet and later died of his injuries. While this is a heartbreaking story, are Sally and Mala bad dogs? No, they just have super-high prey drives and shouldn't be living with a small dog. Perhaps it would be best if they didn't live with any other dogs. Sally and Mala had never shown any aggression to the Pug or any other dogs before this incident. It was completely unexpected.

The family of the dogs decided the only safe thing they could do was to re-home Mala and Sally, thereby potentially saving the life of their other Pug. Did Mala and Sally's owner know this could have happened? Of course not—otherwise they never would have left the dogs alone together. These dogs were all older and had lived together for many years, so the owners didn't think there was anything to worry about. This is a prime example of why you may always want to use a fence as a barrier between your dog and another. There is never one right choice because each dog acts differently. This is why it is essential for you, as an owner, to be aware of what *could* happen and to know how to react accordingly.

Choose the situations into which you decide to take your dog-aggressive dog. Where I live, everyone wants to have their dogs off leash. We have miles of hiking trails, parks, and walking paths that allow dogs. The biggest problem my clients have is when they are walking their dog-aggressive dog on leash and they encounter an off-leash dog. See Chapter 8 for help with this. One of the heartaches of owning a dog-aggressive dog is that you cannot take your dog off leash on hiking trails or in parks. It's just not the responsible thing to do and it's not fair to other dog owners either. However, you can teach your dog to behave in these situations (see Chapter 3) so you can have a dog with which you can hike and walk

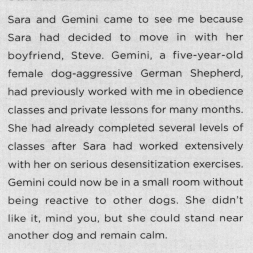

SIDEBARK

Sara and Gemini

Sara and Gemini came to see me because Sara had decided to move in with her boyfriend, Steve. Gemini, a five-year-old female dog-aggressive German Shepherd, had previously worked with me in obedience classes and private lessons for many months. She had already completed several levels of classes after Sara had worked extensively with her on serious desensitization exercises. Gemini could now be in a small room without being reactive to other dogs. She didn't like it, mind you, but she could stand near another dog and remain calm.

When Sara told me she was moving in with Steve and Steve's three-year-old Boston Terrier, Thelma, I was both concerned and hopeful. I suggested Sara bring both dogs to my training center where we could do the introductions. We had Thelma come into the room first and gave her a chance to wander around and get used to the place. After about fifteen minutes, we brought Gemini in on the other side of a wooden railing fence in my training center. We had one dog on each side of the fence with the respective owners standing nearby. I was in the main part of the training center, next to Thelma. Gemini, having had so much desensitization training, immediately looked to Sara for guidance and treats. She had no interest in Thelma.

This was a good start, but I wanted to see what the dogs would do together. We waited.

continued on next page

SIDEBARK

Sara and Gemini (continued)

Thelma ran up and down the railing trying to get Gemini's attention, but with a bit of hesitation as she was able to sense Gemini's dominance. I had Sara reward Gemini with a few small hot dog slices because Gemini was being so good.

After about two minutes, which actually felt like a long time, Gemini turned her attention to Thelma and let out a low growl through the fence. Thelma backed up about three or four feet and stood there, looking at Gemini. Next, the dogs ran up and down the fence line assessing each other. Gemini growled at first, just for a few seconds, but quickly began to relax. This was a good sign. We allowed the two females to run up and down the fence for about five minutes. At one point, Thelma dropped her front end into a play bow, to which Gemini replied with a growl and then a retreat to Sara. We rewarded the retreat because this is a good behavior—it's not aggression!

Thelma barked a few times, and Gemini became interested in her and went up to the fence and sniffed. The two dogs ran back and forth and began to show a curious interest in each other. Gemini stopped growling and began to relax. We were all pleased and again rewarded Gemini with treats for relaxing. After about fifteen minutes the two dogs began to lose interest in each other altogether.

The next step was to bring Gemini into the main room, where Thelma was, with each dog dragging a leash. Both owners were nervous, but I remained calm. I had a good feeling about this. The two dogs met nose to nose and Gemini appeared surprised at being able to actually make contact with another dog. The dogs were fine! Gemini was tense and holding her breath a great deal but did not growl or show aggression of any type. This was the first time Gemini had been allowed to make contact with another dog since she had injured a dog a few years earlier. Sara and Steve were thrilled. I was happy because they were happy. We continued to let Gemini and Thelma run around and sniff the training center and get to know each other. About twenty minutes went by and soon the dogs showed no interest in each other. At this point, Sara and Steve were ready to leave. Because we knew our attention wouldn't fully be on the dogs, we took each dog's leash and moved them away from each other. We put Gemini in her car and finished up our lesson.

My suggestion to Sara and Steve was to go somewhere for a walk with the two dogs. Let them be side by side but not in a room together. Then in a day or two to try the whole thing over again by using Steve's fenced yard as the barrier between the dogs (Sara and Steve were not living together yet). I further suggested that once Sara and Steve moved in together that the dogs never be left unattended together, even though they seemed like they were going to be fine with each other. It was better to be safe than sorry.

on bike paths with a lot of slow, consistent training.

If you do want to introduce two dogs and you do not have the option of a fence between them, you can do the same type of introduction with a baby gate between the dogs. This would obviously mean you are in someone's house with the two dogs. Be careful setting this up, as you don't want the dogs to make contact with each other before the gate goes up. And because baby gates aren't the strongest contraptions in the world, have leashes on the dogs so you can pull them apart if need be. The scenario is the same as if you had a fence between the dogs. Let them say what they want to say to each other without interfering. Use the leashes only if one of the dogs is going to jump or knock over the baby gate.

Neutral Territory Introductions

One of the questions that will often arise when doing these types of dog introductions is at whose house should the joining take place? Ideally, you want to conduct them on neutral territory. If you don't have a fenced yard, ask a friend or neighbor if you can use theirs for a little while instead. If both dogs have a fenced yard, do it at the house of the less aggressive dog. If neither dog has a fenced yard and you are doing it inside one of your houses, again, do it at the house of the less aggressive or non-aggressive dog. You want to give the home court advantage to the more

submissive of the two dogs to reduce the risk of territorial aggression on the part of the more aggressive dog.

Introductions on neutral territory even the playing field by leaving less of a chance of having one of the dogs behave more aggressively than the other. *Credit: Sarah D. Todd*

If you have a situation that involves more than two dogs, conduct the introductions one at a time so the pack mentality doesn't work against you. Always start with pairings, and then combine the dogs together after all of the dogs have met each other in pairs. Add the least aggressive to the most aggressive dogs in that order. You don't want the more aggressive dogs to gang up on the more submissive dog. Be careful if you are doing this with three or more dogs. Your fight will be worse if there is any pack mentality going on.

At my house, when I am introducing a new boarder to the household, I lock up or crate all the dogs. Then the new dog comes in and gets a chance to sniff around and check out the house. Then I put one or two of the established dogs with the new one. Once they become comfortable with each other, I add in another one or two dogs. I do this until all the dogs are mixing nicely together.

Boarding Your Dog When You Go Away

Today, quite a few kennels allow dogs to roam around freely. However, most dog-aggressive dogs must stay in more traditional kennels; day-cares and in-home boarding will not be able to accommodate a dog-aggressive dog. Personally, I cannot board aggressive dogs because my dogs live communally in my home and there are no kennels or separation. While I'm not set up to board aggressive dogs, I can refer clients to people who are, as many traditional facilities have separate runs for the dogs. You shouldn't feel bad if you must board your dog in a traditional facility. I worked in a kennel for many years, and if you find one that is well run and where the animals are looked after with love and kindness, then your dog will be okay.

Other options are available. You can try to find a house sitter, and there are lots of pet sitting services available these days. Call your veterinarian's office, your local shelter, or a pet supply store to get references for a pet sitter or a reputable kennel in your area.

Dog-Aggressive Dog Case Studies

The following examples are a few actual case studies of dog-aggressive dogs.

Nala and Bowen

In December 2006, I met with a couple and their two dogs, Nala and Bowen. Nala was a three-year-old Border Collie mix and Bowen was a three-year-old purebred Border Collie. Rena and Bob had adopted Nala from a local rescue group six months previous to the consult. Bowen had been purchased as a twelve-week-old puppy from a breeder.

The couple came to me because Nala had been displaying aggression to other dogs by growling, snarling, and lunging when she saw the new dog. Prior to Nala's arrival, Bowen had not shown dog aggression except when on leash. Nala's aggression was one of the more interesting cases I have seen.

My executive director, Sam, and I evaluated Nala with other dogs to see what type of aggression she had and if she was going to be able to be rehabilitated. First, we observed Nala's behavior with Boon, a large hound mix. We left Bowen in another room to see how Nala would behave without his influence. Nala was excited to see Boon—whining and giving a loose, easy tail wag. She showed no signs of aggression.

Next, we brought Bowen into the room, and Nala's behavior changed. When we allowed her to approach Boon she immediately jumped up and grabbed Boon by the neck. Of course, we separated the dogs. We took Bowen out of the room and Nala was once again fine with Boon.

After that we evaluated Nala with my Shiloh Shepherd, Kobe. Nala and Kobe greeted each other on leash and were fine with each other. Kobe is a good judge of dog character and will let me know when another dog has aggression. Kobe did a play bow to Nala and Nala responded in kind.

We then tried Nala with a female mix, Trout, who is a fairly dominant dog. Trout growled at Nala and Nala respected the growl, backed down, and showed submission.

What's interesting about this case is that Nala's aggression was clearly related to her relationship with Bowen. Nala and Bowen are great with each other, but Nala would not be able to be introduced to other dogs with Bowen present. The options to Rena and Bob were to desensitize Nala so she could be managed in the presence of other dogs, to keep Nala away from other dogs, or to return Nala to the rescue group from which she came.

Rena and Bob's lifestyle was called into question here, because they enjoy having their dogs around friends' and family's dogs. They had a difficult choice to make, and left the consult with much on their minds. They ended up keeping both the dogs, but stopped taking them with them to gatherings. They felt bad separating the dogs, so they left them both home when they went to family events.

Nala was an interesting case of dog to dog aggression because she was fine with Bowen and could possibly have been fine with other dogs in his absence. The desensitization program would be effective in allowing Rena and Bob to walk down their country road with Nala calmly at their side.

Ben and Alice

Ben was an extremely active six-year-old yellow Labrador Retriever who was being fostered by Alice at her home. Ben also lived with Jasper, Corby, and Boomer, Alice's three resident mixed breed dogs. When Ben first came to live with Alice, he was pushy with her dogs but after some posturing and growling from the three dogs, Ben learned his place and began to respect the other dogs' space.

Alice came to me because she was thinking about keeping Ben, but she said he had issues greeting other dogs. She wanted him evaluated for dog aggression to see if he was truly aggressive or not. Immediately I learned that he *was* an interesting dog, definitely unlike any other dog I had met. For starters, he would "mark" every place he could in my office. This was typical behavior of an unaltered or neutered-late dog (but we eventually had to put him on leash to stop the peeing extravaganza). We were guessing that Ben was neutered late, but didn't know for sure as he was already altered when he came to the rescue.

I spent about an hour getting to know Ben and Alice and hearing Alice's concerns. It is typical for me to spend this hour with people before I introduce other dogs. Alice described Ben as exuberant, overactive, and in your face. She said when it came to other dogs, he was "intrusive and rude," particularly at first. Alice has lots of visitors with dogs to her house, and one of her main concerns was that she wanted to live with a dog that would get along with others.

After our intake, I brought in my dog, Wyatt, and asked Alice to simply hold Ben at about a half leash length and just observe his behavior. This is how I usually conduct my evaluations. I want to see the dog with another dog, no intervening, no talking to the dogs, just watching. Ben barked liked crazy, but kept a loose body posture with his tail parallel to the floor and medium-pitched vocalizations—noisy, but not acting dominant or aggressive.

Next I brought in another dog, Jigs. Ben reacted the same way. As I brought Jigs closer, Jigs' tail went up but Ben's did not. As soon as they were close enough to make contact, Ben put his head over Jigs' withers. Jigs growled and Ben backed off. I also brought in my dog, Kobe, and expected something a bit more dominant out of Ben, as Alice had said Ben was worse with large, dominant males—exactly what Kobe is. Strangely, Ben behaved the same with Kobe as he had with Jigs.

I watched Ben with interest because everything about Ben said to me, *aroused, dominant male.* He seemed aroused both sexually and emotionally, but his body language made him come across as relaxed. I found Ben odd because dogs with his MO usually act outright tough and dominant, if not aggressive.

I concluded that Ben was like a body builder—big and well-muscled. If a body builder walked into the room, you would know he was tough and strong. He wouldn't need to flex his muscles to prove that he was a powerful man. Even if the body builder held his head low and his shoulders hunched over, one would see this was not a person to mess with. That's how I saw Ben. He was a big, tough, charged up dog who displayed non-dominant body language—that is, until he actually made contact with the other dog by putting his head over that other dog. But even with doing so, he still managed to maintain a calm demeanor.

This is quite unusual dog behavior. While they often have mixed emotions, and their bodies will show this, I was unaccustomed to seeing a dog act relaxed when he was very dominant. It's true that the most dominant dogs fight the least, but they still exhibit serious body language when exposed to a new dog. They stand up tall to show they're boss. Ben wagged his tail low and whined after the initial barking, but it was clear to me that the other dogs saw a body builder in this dog and were simply intimidated by him. After a few more months of both debating and training, Alice decided to keep Ben.

Grace and Teton

Grace, my Border Collie, fought on occasion only with other dominant females that came to live with me. Aside from those few occasions, she was always good with other dogs. In Chapter 4, I described the situation between Grace and Tara, the Golden that came to live with me. Well, Grace had issues with another dog, Teton. Teton, a spayed female yellow Labrador Retriever, lived with my family and me for a few months. In the beginning, Grace and Teton got along well, even playing together in the big, fenced yard. We hiked together daily with both dogs off leash and they were fine on all the hikes, never having a problem with each other.

One day, in the middle of a blizzardy January, I was hiking up a small mountain near my house. It's a beautiful, tree-filled hike along an old logging trail up the side of the mountain. The hike takes about forty minutes to get up to the top, and then in the winter, one can sled down the trail at warp speed and almost fly! It's a really fun activity for the dogs and I to do on a cold winter day. I was hiking with Grace, Brody, Teton, and a few other boarding dogs. All the dogs were off leash and they were running and having a blast. I hiked to the top of the mountain and prepared myself to sled down. I had to add a neck warmer and ski goggles for the trip downhill.

I started down the trail on my cheap plastic sled with the dogs whooping and barking in excitement. They go nuts just before we start sledding, and even are a bit crazed as we sled down the hill. The speed arouses them and incites their prey drive. This may be what caused Grace and Teton to break into a fight. I am not sure exactly what started it, as I was sledding down the mountain when it happened. But I looked over and saw the two of them thrashing each other around and grabbing and pinning each other to the ground. They were rolling and tumbling in the deep snow off the side of the trail. I leapt off my sled and tried to grab one of the dogs by the collar. Nothing happened. I grabbed the other dog by the collar, not caring if I got bitten. But

still nothing happened. The two dogs were latched onto each other and neither dog was going to let go. I screamed and hit at them and tried desperately to pull them apart, but to no avail. Fortunately, the other dogs didn't join in but waited patiently as I tried in vain to separate the two girls. No matter what I tried, I couldn't get them apart. I waited. And waited. For what seemed like an eternity I tried unsuccessfully to get them to stop fighting. I was scared and anxious and I thought with all that adrenalin I should have been able to get them to split up. I couldn't. I just had to keep trying and to wait. I was yelling and hollering but it did no good.

After several minutes of tussling, Teton, with her sixty-five pounds, pinned Grace's thirty-two pounds. Grace was no match for Teton because of the size difference. When two dogs are evenly matched for dominance, the bigger dog will usually win the fight, but I really couldn't tell if Grace was trying to submit or not. Teton had Grace on her back in the snow and both dogs were biting at each other. Grace didn't let go of her grip or look like she would relinquish power to Teton. This continued for several minutes while I anxiously tried to get them to stop. Finally, after what seemed like an hour but was probably several minutes, the two dogs broke apart and I was able to leash Teton and verbally keep Grace away from Teton by putting Grace in a down-stay. Grace's obedience was impeccable, except in this rare situation when she was fighting.

After the dogs were split up, I assessed both of them for damage. I was expecting to have to carry one or both of the dogs down the mountain and then rush to the vet's office. The first thing I realized was that I didn't see any blood. I had seen a lot of fur flying, but no blood. I carefully inspected the dogs. Neither dog had a mark on her. I was shocked and amazed but *so* relieved. They were both panting and wet with saliva, but there was not a single sign of a puncture wound or tear anywhere. Exhausted but thankful, I walked down the mountain with Teton on leash. Grace kept her distance and didn't try to pick a fight with Teton.

Like with Tara, the Golden, Teton went to live with an employee for the rest of her time boarding. And for the rest of Teton's life, she had to board elsewhere because once dogs fight like that you just can't risk putting them together again. Interestingly, they might have been fine together, but I was not willing to take the chance that they would have another fight like that one. It was too scary, even though neither dog was injured in the fight.

Willy and Dewey

My Dog to Dog Communication class is designed for dogs that have known aggression issues with other dogs. It is a five-week course, with two hours at each meeting. The first two weeks are attended by the humans only, and we cover much of the information that is in earlier chapters of this book. Also, the dog owners have a homework assignment to do between week one and week two of the course. They are to safely observe their dog in the presence of another dog, having the dogs make no contact with each other, just observing their dog's body language much like I do when I consult with people at my training center. During the second week of class, I have the owners share the information they gathered when observing their dog. I also collect notes and pictures if there are any. I love it when owners take pictures of their dogs communicating with other dogs. Even though it's at a distance, it's still great body language to see.

After the second week's class when I have all the information about the dogs, I sit down and review it. I then make pairings of how the dogs are going to be introduced to each other during the third week of class. I prefer to do "like" pairings in the class so dogs are evenly matched when they meet. In no way do I allow the dogs to hurt or negatively impact the other dogs in class. I am trying to find out whether each dog will regain some of the social skills he learned in their earlier life, if allowed to actually "talk" to another dog. Remember, all dogs, with the exception of singleton puppies, learn some amount of communication from their littermates. I find that many dogs, when given the chance to communicate with another dog without owner interference, actually de-escalate in their communication and can be fine with each other.

When you own an aggressive dog, you can't just let it approach other dogs at random. Most owners spend a tremendous amount of energy keeping other dogs away from their dog. So in this class, people get a chance to see what their dogs will say to another dog. These pairings have a typical pattern. I do a lot of preparation with the owners to get them ready for the dogs meeting each other. The dog's preparation comes from being trained to wear the muzzle, as all interactions are done with the muzzles on. But the owners are understandably quite nervous about what is going to happen at class. I literally get the class to sing a song, any song. We usually sing "Happy Birthday." The singing gets the class to breathe and relax a little bit. Then I hand out lollipops to everyone to bring down the stress level further and to keep people breathing. Next, I have one person bring in his dog, sit on one side of the room, and put the muzzle on his dog. Then I have the second owner muzzle her dog outside the classroom and bring the dog in when she's ready. I have one owner sit on each side of the room, about 50 feet away from each other. When the owners are ready, I have them drop their leashes and let the dogs go. Normally, the dogs run toward the center of the room and begin to say something to each other.

In one class, I had a neutered male brown Newfoundland named Willy and a neutered male Leonberger named Dewey—two very large dogs that were about the same age and both seemed to have dominance aggression with other dogs. I thought they would be a perfect pairing. So we brought them into the training center and started with one dog sitting on each

side of the room. My job is to interpret body language and explain to the owners what the dogs are saying to one another, first while they are across the room from each other and then when they come together.

Willy and Dewey flew into the center of the room growling, barking (as best they could with muzzles on), and attempting to attack each other. They tussled and tossed each other around with their powerful legs and bodies. They thrashed their heads at each other, both attempting to gain the upper hand. As they went at each other, I explained to the humans what the posturing meant. The raised paws on each other's backs, the deep-throated vocalizations, the body slamming, each dog trying to be the dominant one. It seemed like an eternity, but the fight continued for only a minute or two. Both dogs vied for dominance, and being the same size, neither dog was getting anywhere.

Just as I was ready to call it a draw and separate the dogs, Willy made one huge slam that sent Dewey away with fervor. All of a sudden, the dogs were quiet, Willy walking in a dominant fashion toward Dewey who was now cowering in the corner. All the while, the owners were being guided through a round of "Happy Birthday" by one of my assistants to try and keep everyone calm. The dogs had fought and it had ended with Willy as champion. What I think Willy learned in the fight was that he could use his body to say his piece and it would be respected. As soon as Dewey relinquished power to Willy, Willy calmed down.

This also taught us that Willy is a very dominant dog that needed to be controlled in all situations. The muzzled introduction let us see that Willy would not be safe with other dogs. The altercation taught Dewey that it benefited him to submit and that losing a fight wasn't so bad. Those few minutes when the fight was going on were very tense for everyone, but they let us observe the dogs and taught them how to communicate properly.

Willy, the Newfie, went on to continue his training and earned high titles in the American Kennel Club's obedience competitions. His owner worked hard with him, teaching him to behave perfectly in the presence of other dogs. Willy could never have playtime and certainly would never be allowed at a dog park, but he was able to learn complete control under all circumstances. Dewey, a family companion, went on to socialize with the neighbor's dogs without incident after the Dog to Dog Communication class. Dewey learned that submitting was beneficial and was possible. Before the class, all Dewey knew was to be dominant over other dogs. With Willy, he learned how to be submissive and that if he was submissive, other dogs might respect that. Prior to the class, Dewey's owners had always had problems with neighborhood dogs roaming into their yard. It seemed Willy "cured" Dewey of his dominance aggression and allowed Dewey to regain some of his early learned social behaviors. Dewey and Willy both lived long, happy lives with their respective families.

Chapter 8   Inevitable Encounters

Country Roads and City Streets

Brutus is a three-year-old neutered male Newfoundland/Border Collie mix. He came to see me with his owner, John, because when John walks Brutus down his country road, Brutus shows aggression toward every dog he sees. You might think living in the country exempts you from encountering other dogs, but I live in what some consider to be the middle of nowhere, and I see neighbors' dogs every day. John wanted to help Brutus change his attitude with the dogs in his area. He didn't need Brutus to play with other dogs; he just wanted him to be able to walk down their country road without barking, lunging, and growling at every dog he saw.

When Brutus came to see me, he knew sit, lie down, and a good solid eye contact from prior training with John. I did the intake and then exposed Brutus to my dogs to see how he would act. I had no doubt he would behave poorly, but I wanted to see for myself how bad he was or wasn't. First I brought in Wyatt, as I usually do, and Brutus went berserk, barking and pulling at the end of his leash. Initially, I had told John not to do anything but observe Brutus when I brought Wyatt in. After Wyatt came in and I saw Brutus's behavior, I asked John to try getting Brutus to sit. Wyatt was way too close for Brutus's obedience to work, so I quickly took Wyatt out and came back in to talk to John. I was not surprised that Brutus could not respond to the sit command under the stress of having a dog so close (Wyatt was about fifteen feet away).

Next I reviewed basic training exercises with John and explained how to increase distractions slowly. I told him to seek out training areas where he could control the distance of the other dog. I described parking lot (desensitization) training, and how he could use the peanut butter container to guide Brutus down the road when he saw other dogs. I explained that during the training process, when he was out walking Brutus for his bathroom breaks, he would have to deal with Brutus's carrying on but as he did the desensitization training Brutus would get calmer and calmer with the strange dogs. I also suggested that John carry a container of concentrated breath spray with him, and to spray Brutus if his aggression went over the top. I am happy to say that I just received an e-mail from John letting me know that the peanut butter cup was a huge success, Brutus's critical distance is down to across the road, and their walks are much happier for both of them.

Walking down a country road or a sidewalk can be a difficult task for any dog owner. Whether your dog is friendly and trying to pull you over out of excitement or whether your dog is aggressive and pulling you toward the other dog because he wants to kill it, it can be hard to control your dog. If your dog is friendly, I highly recommend you enroll it in an obedience class with a local trainer who uses positive reinforcement training. Taking a class can be one of the easiest ways to expose your dog to others and to get some training at the same time. In a basic class, you should learn loose-leash walking or heel, sit, down, stay, look, come, and more. Basic behavioral issues are usually covered in a beginner obedience class as well. The benefits of taking a six- or eight-week course can last a lifetime in helping you have basic control over your dog.

If you can't find the time for a class or if your dog is dog-aggressive, you may need to do the training at home. For walking down the street, the most important exercises are heel and look. If you teach your dog to heel at your side, in the face of any distraction, you can safely control your dog under most circumstances. If you combine this with the "look" exercise, your dog will be a star and definitely heel down the street even with other dogs in the vicinity. You don't need to keep your dog at a heel at all times, just when you see another dog. If she's walking at the end of the leash, call her to come and then ask her to heel, and off you go past the other dog.

Hiking Trails

Hiking trails are another common place to see other dogs, and in Vermont where I live, everyone wants to hike with their dogs off leash. Just today I was at a park called Indian Brook Reservoir in Essex, Vermont, and I was with two friends. Between us we were hiking with a dozen dogs. Now, fortunately we were at a place where we are allowed to have our dogs off leash. And even with twelve dogs, we maintained control. How did we do this? Well, each of the dogs had been individually trained to behave off leash. Each dog, one at a time, had been taught to come when called and to heel off leash. When we see another dog on the trail we do a massive group "Come," and all the dogs miraculously come running back to us. It's quite a sight to see all these dogs respond like a circling school of fish. They come running back and we promptly put the dogs into a sit or down-stay. Then the other person's dog can safely walk by us and our pack and when it's over, off we go. We release the dogs and they are free to run again.

The only safe and conscionable way to hike with your dog off leash is to have a perfect recall, or to be somewhere that you know you won't see any other dogs, which is uncommon. Even in remote places in Vermont, if it's public, we see other dogs and people. And it's not any nicer to have your dog run up to a person than it is to another dog. So spend the time training and get that perfect recall. It's doable; it just takes a lot of time.

If you are hiking with your dog off leash and you see another dog, call your dog to you. Put on the leash so you have some control over your dog. This is usually easiest, although if you have a solid stay you could use that. I find it easiest to stop moving and control my dog while standing still. I like to use a container full of peanut butter to hold my dog's attention on me, although if you have a dog park dog you may just be able to stand there and wait while the other dog passes. Either way,

keep your dog focused on you while the other dog goes by. Then, if appropriate, take your dog's leash off and let her run again. Kate Carter, managing editor of *Vermont Sports* magazine, wrote an article in the April 2007 edition titled "Mastering Canine Trail Manners." Carter writes:

Last fall, while hiking on the Lake Mansfield Trail to Taylor Lodge [in Vermont] with Phoebe and Brewster [her two Border Collies], I could see four people coming down the trail toward us. I called both dogs and moved to the side to let the other hikers pass by. We exchanged greetings and chatted briefly, and all the while I was giving my dogs treats for sitting by my side. Someone commented on all the goodies Brewster and Phoebe were getting. "Does this go on for the entire hike?" he asked. "Only when we see other people," I explained. "That way their focus is on me, not on you." They thought that was brilliant and just about the cleverest thing they'd ever heard. I was surprised at their reaction. It seemed so obvious to me, but then I remembered that not everyone knows the value of treats, or the philosophy of positive training.

Make sure you practice lots of recalls when you are hiking with your dog. There are a few reasons for this. One is because practice makes perfect, and the more you call your dog to come the better she will be at doing it. The other reason is that you don't only want to call your dog to come when there is a huge distraction, or your dog will start to dislike coming to you. If you are always calling the dog away from something interesting, the recall will become a difficult exercise. So practice it often, and use lots of really high-quality, yummy treats. As I have said before, no minimum-wage treats if you want that amazing recall. Hot dog slices, cheese, steak, chicken, or sandwich meats are called for here. Keep practicing that recall until it is perfect, and then you can have your dog off leash.

The Veterinarian's Office

Another place where running into dogs is inevitable is at the veterinarian's office. If you own a dog park dog, this can be a breeze and can be a fun time for you and your dog. You do want to respect other dogs' space and give them some room. You don't know why the other dog is there and he could be sick. But if you check with the other dog's owner and all is well, then let your dog greet and sniff while you wait for the vet. This can be a great little socialization opportunity for your dog.

If you own a dog with issues, the vet's office can be particularly difficult for a few reasons. The first is that vets' waiting rooms are usually a relatively small space. Second, if your dog is sick you can't always use treats to train her. Prior training helps tremendously. If you haven't trained your dog and you have to go to the vet, the only thing you may be able to

do is to reel your dog in on a tight leash and hope for the best—if you cannot use food because your dog is sick. If you are going to the vet's office for something like an annual exam and your dog is feeling fine, grab a container full of peanut butter and try sticking that in your dog's face. Guide her through the waiting room and into the exam room with the peanut butter container almost attached to her nose.

NOTE It can take some practice for you to be able to feed and walk at the same time, and for your dog to eat and follow at the same time, but just be patient. Eventually you'll get the hang of it if you follow the exercises in Chapter 3 on avoiding distractions.

If you know you have a vet appointment in several weeks or you're reading this because you just had a bad experience at the vet's office and you want the next trip to go better, don't worry—you have some time to train. Go through the exercises in Chapter 3 and begin to train your dog to heel, sit, down, look, and stay. These are the basic exercises you need to control your dog under any circumstances while in the face of dog distractions. On the scale of distractions, other dogs rate as one of the highest, whether your dog is friendly or not. Regardless of how your dog feels about the other dogs, there is a good chance she will want to pull you over to the other dog in the waiting room.

Dan Hament, co-owner of Richmond Animal Hospital in Richmond, Vermont, thinks the best approach is to make sure the waiting room is empty or to use an alternative entrance. "A tight leash for a few seconds is not the end of the world and works very well in most circumstances. If you can alert the veterinarian's staff that you have a dog-aggressive dog, it allows them to help the owner to determine the best course of action. It's allowing the professionals to advise the owner, and isn't that what you want from your veterinarian in the first place?"

Recently I took Oscar to the veterinarian's office. When I got there, I went in without Oscar to see if the waiting room was empty. When I saw that no one was there, I went to the car and got him. I walked him through the waiting room and straight into the exam room. When our appointment was over, I asked the vet to check the waiting room to see if there were any dogs there. There weren't, so I was able to walk out without any problems.

Had there been dogs in the waiting room I would have had two options. One, there is another door I could have gone out that leads straight to the parking lot—the only problem is that the snow was about three feet deep outside the door. Two, I could have used my container full of peanut butter and walked Oscar past the dogs with the peanut butter in his face. Oscar is so food-motivated that this works well. He may occasionally move away from the food and growl, but mostly he'll follow the

SIDEBARK

Josh and Julia

Josh was a four-year-old neutered male Labradoodle who had been purchased from a breeder. In the past eight months Josh had had chronic ear infections and was frequently being seen by his veterinarian. His owner, Julia, brought him to see me because on several of these occasions, Josh had to hang out in the waiting room while Julia waited for the appointment. Josh loved other dogs, but had become increasingly unmanageable in the waiting room.

Julia frequented the dog park with Josh, so his time with other dogs was normally unstructured and free playtime. Unfortunately, Josh thought the time in the waiting room should be playtime as well. It got to the point that he was hurting Julia's arm as she tried to restrain him. Josh had never been to an obedience class, but knew how to sit and lie down and was well mannered in his home. The only real problem Julia was having with Josh was at her vet's office, and the vet had recommended they come to see me for some help.

I evaluated Josh with my dogs. First, I brought in Wyatt, my usual primary tester with other dogs. Josh wiggled and wagged and tried his hardest to get to Wyatt. Since Wyatt is blind, I don't allow other dogs to make face-to-face contact with him. I just keep them at a distance from each other to see how my clients' dogs will behave. Next I

continued on next page

Josh and Julia (continued)

brought in Kobe, and Josh again was uncontrollable—squirming and twisting about excitedly. Josh showed zero aggression and was all play in his behavior. Kobe's greeting behaviors were less playful, so I didn't put them together. Last, I brought in Jigs, who loves to play with other dogs. I first introduced them at a distance so I could observe Josh's behavior. It was clear by now that Josh didn't have an unfriendly bone in his body. He loved other dogs and simply wanted to play! I let Jigs go all the way up to Josh and let them interact. They did a typical sniff and groin smell, and then Josh went into a play bow and initiated play with Jigs. Jigs reciprocated by tossing his back end toward Josh and then play bowing. The dogs quickly began to wrestle with each other and had a blast playing. We let them play for about fifteen minutes and then we put Jigs back into the front office.

I gave Julia the good news that Josh seemed to have no aggression issues with other dogs, and I thought all her problems in the vet's office were because Josh was used to always being allowed to play with other dogs. Julia told me she was willing to do what it took to be able to better manage Josh in the vet's office, but that she wasn't interested in any training beyond that. I showed Julia how to get Josh to heel and look. I demonstrated this with Josh in my office. Next I showed Julia how effective a container of peanut butter container was at holding Josh's attention. Josh would readily sit for the peanut butter.

So with the peanut butter in Julia's hand, I brought Wyatt into the consult room and kept him at a distance. I had Julia feed, feed, feed, and to her amazement Josh kept his nose in the food and didn't try to get to Wyatt. We repeated this same exercise with Kobe and then with Jigs. Each time I brought a new dog into the room, Julia fed and praised Josh and he ate away at the food. We had to refill the cup between each dog but that was fine.

NOTE If you use a lot of food in training, skip or reduce your dog's next regular meal. It is fine to use food for training—you just don't want your dog to get fat in the process! (Consult with your vet regarding the proper weight for your dog.)

We were happy to find that Josh was easily distracted by the food, and I was confident that when Josh had his next vet appointment, Julia would be able to better manage him. I encouraged her to teach the heel and look so that she could occupy Josh with some other behaviors, and also to make coming and going into the vet's office easier. But I thought the peanut butter was going to make the biggest difference in his behavior. Julia left with a happy Josh at her side.

food. If he does growl I either ignore him or use my stop word and the concentrated breath spray. Usually, since I know the situation is short lived and I will be out of there quickly, I just use the peanut butter container and try to zip through the waiting room.

Chapter 9  **Chosen Encounters**

og parks, doggie daycare centers, and family picnics are just a few of the places one might encounter dogs. Here in Vermont, everyone loves to take their dogs with them on outings, so you are more than likely to see other dogs. Most cities now have fenced dog parks where you can take your dog for some much-needed exercise and play.

Dog Parks

There are pros and cons to bringing your pup to a dog park. The good stuff: They are a fantastic place to get your dog exercised and tired out. There is nothing like dog to dog play to exhaust your canine companion. And it's easy on the owner, too. You can drink a cup of coffee and talk with your dog-loving friends. You don't need to do anything but dress for the weather and enjoy the day. Your dog will do everything else. Dog parks are perfect spots for a good exercise session for your four-legged friend.

Many dogs *love* to play with other dogs, and this is another excellent reason to take your dog to the dog park. Most dogs make best friends at dog parks and they look forward to these visits quite a lot.

Jane and her two-year-old Collie mix, Cassie, visit the dog park on a regular basis. When asked why she takes Cassie to the dog park almost every day, Jane said, "We just love it there. We both have friends and have a blast hanging out. Well, I love hanging out and Cassie loves to romp with the other dogs. It's a great place."

Checking Out the Other Canines

When taking your dog to the dog park, it's wise to stand outside the fence and observe for a few minutes. Check out the dogs in the park. Are they playing nicely? Do you see any fights occurring? Are there very large dogs, and if so are they playing well? Does it look like a good situation for your dog to join? Take enough time to really watch the dogs interact with each other.

Enter the park and try to give your dog some space from the other dogs when you first walk in. If your dog is mobbed by the other dogs it may be overwhelming for her. If it's possible, let your dog stay a small distance from the other dogs and let her approach the pack when she's ready. *Never* immediately walk into the throng of other dogs. Give your dog a minute to warm up to being at the park and assess things for herself.

NOTE Don't worry if your dog takes a while to want to go into the pack. She'll let you know when she's ready. If, on the other hand, your dog wants to race into the group of dogs at the park, and then by all means, let her.

You don't need or want to restrain your dog when she enters the park. Take off her leash as quickly as possible so she is free to communicate on her own without the restraint or interference of the leash. Remember, leashes can cause issues because of the tension humans put on them. The dog feels unsafe because she's unable to display proper body language and maintain the safe distance she might want to keep from the other dogs. So always remember to take your dog's leash off quickly.

Why Dog Parks Have a Bad Rap

Many dog trainers and other dog professionals think poorly of dog parks. This is because there are often unruly, unfriendly dogs at the dog park. Few dog parks are monitored by anyone. A great deal of bad dog behavior goes on in dog parks. Many fights occur; dogs get injured or aggressed upon regularly. No one stops bad behavior. (And I say this with the knowledge that I allow or believe in more dog displays of various types of behavior than many people.)

It's obvious that many dog owners believe in the positive aspects of dog parks; an abundance of these parks have sprung up all over the country within the last ten years. However, the people who are against them have good reason. I have spoken with many veterinarians who have stitched up dogs from injuries received at dog parks. While most vets understand the need for exercise, they don't always feel that dog parks are the place to get it. They would rather see you run with your dog or play fetch or take your dog swimming.

Dr. Anne Bazilwich says dog caretakers should be aware that injuries can occur at any time and at any place. "Although accidents and injuries may occur at a dog park, I firmly believe similar [accidents] may occur anywhere and in any situation. I had a patient who was injured in his own enclosed backyard by another dog who was loose [outside the fence] and managed to find a way into the yard. We do our best to protect our dogs, but we cannot keep them in a bubble. They need exercise—they thrive on exercise—and interaction with healthy, playful dogs is essential."

Most municipalities have dog parks because the dog-owning public loves them. Just be careful, and if there is an aggressive dog at the dog park, leave. It's not worth it to run the risk of injury to your dog. I hear countless stories of such and such being the "bad" dog at the park and the owner doesn't recognize or doesn't care that their dog is being aggressive.

Playing by the Rules

Few, if any, real rules stand at dog parks. There are usually lists of rules on a sign when you walk in, but the actual policing is left to the dog owners—many of whom are uncomfortable with the idea of telling someone they shouldn't be at the park.

I recently received an e-mail from a client who was at the dog park working on rehabilitating her spirited dog. She said her dog, Jackson, was playing there when a Siberian Husky came in and started posturing at many of the dogs. The Husky approached Jackson and mounted him. Jackson corrected the Husky for mounting and a fight ensued. Jackson and his owner ended up leaving the park because the Husky owner didn't want to leave.

Sometimes behavior is occurring that owners don't realize is not healthy for their dog. I tell people to trust their instincts. If something feels wrong, it probably is. Don't leave your dog to fend for himself if there is an aggressive dog at the park. You need to intervene and keep your dog safe. Come back another day if necessary. It's better to be safe than sorry.

When to Call it Quits

Lots of mounting happens at dog parks. This can be an iffy behavior. Some dogs tolerate it, and others do not. You know your dog. If another dog keeps mounting your dog, you may want to leave. If your dog doesn't mind being mounted, then you don't need to worry about it. But always trust yourself; if it doesn't feel right, it probably isn't. Some dogs love to body slam each other when they play. Others are more reserved. Some dogs make lots of noise and some dogs are always playing tag. Learn what style of play your dog has and then try to hook him up with others with his style.

Mounting can be a form of play and some dogs tolerate it while others do not. Watch for signs of stress from your dog and take her out of the situation if you sense she wants to get away.
Credit: Detlev Hundsdoerfer

117

Be sure to watch for stress or submissive signs in your dog and leave if necessary. Stress signs can include excessive yawning or scratching or constantly sniffing the ground instead of playing. Another sign could be excessive jumping on the humans. These are not always stress behaviors, but when your dog is supposed to be playing and he's doing these other things, he may be stressed out. Get him out of there if he is. You're better off making a play date with his best friend from the park (at a different location) than staying at the park when your dog is unhappy. Even though your dog may get tired at the park, don't stay because you need your dog exhausted. Stay because your dog loves it there.

Doggie Daycare Centers

As with the dog park, there are several reasons to utilize a doggie daycare center. One is for exercise and another is because your dog just absolutely loves to play with other dogs. A third good reason to use a daycare is because you may have long days at work and you need someone to watch your dog.

Tammy Schey, owner of The Crate Escape, Inc. in Richmond, Vermont, and co-owner of The Crate Escape, too, in South Burlington, Vermont, says, "The main reason people bring their dogs to daycare is to provide their dogs with something fun to do besides sitting around the house day after day waiting for their owners to come home from work." She notes that in the past, dogs were bred and acquired to do specific jobs for their owners. Today they're mainly

acquired for companionship and are largely considered to be part of our families. "It's this bond that we have with our dogs which makes dog daycare as popular as it is today."

What to Look for at Doggie Daycares

A well run dog daycare should be extremely well monitored. There should be at least one staff person for every fifteen or twenty dogs. Often you will see personnel with squirt bottles full of water. They use them to temper mildly inappropriate behaviors. Extremely bad behavior should not be tolerated or allowed. If you see any fights occurring, ask the staff about it, but I would question taking my dog to a daycare where fights occurred regularly.

"Bullying, uncontrolled running, constant humping, and crowding are not allowed," says Schey of her two daycare centers. "Mutual rough play that involves only two dogs is allowed to the extent that neither of the participants is being hurt in any way." She added that this type of play becomes problematic when a third dog (or more) becomes aroused and attempts to get involved. Her staff is trained to distract additional participants or to remove the rough players to an area where they can play without the presence of other dogs. "This is especially important during the midday time when most dogs tend to nap except for the high-energy dogs," she said.

At The Crate Escape, Schey said dogs nap when they want or need to. "Typically the dogs self-regulate their activity: they are active in the early morning upon arrival, activity wanes by late morning, and they get their second wind later in the afternoon." According to Schey, most dogs cue well into this routine and those who resist napping are moved to another area so that those who want to rest can.

How do you know if your dog likes going to daycare? After a few visits, your dog should be pulling you to the door when you go. If that's not happening or if your dog is reluctant to go in, then try a different daycare. Not only should the staff be excited to see your dog, your dog should be happy to be there. If not, stop going.

Questions to Ask the Daycare Staff

Ask lots of questions when you try out a daycare center for your dog. You should definitely find out the answers to the following questions:

1. Is there always a staff person with the dogs or are they left unattended at times?

2. What is the dog-to-staff ratio?

3. Do you let dogs mount each other? If not, how do you stop it?

4. How do you divide up play groups (i.e., by size, play style, age, or breed)?

5. What is your policy on rough play?

6. Are there types of interactions you don't allow and if so, how do you stop them?

7. Do the dogs have nap time and if so, how does this happen (i.e., are they crated)?

8. Can I tour the whole facility?

Personally, I would *never* leave my dogs in a place that would not allow me to see the entire building. I know of one doggie daycare center where the staff won't let people into the back rooms of the building. They claim their insurance company won't allow it. However, a lot of daycares *do* allow people to view the whole facility. Another excuse staff may give you is that it's upsetting to the dogs to have people come in. Again, I wouldn't buy it. Ask to see the whole place before feeling comfortable enough to leave your dog there. If you're told you can't have a full tour, simply find another daycare center. It's that easy, and nowadays there are more than enough great places to which you can take your dog.

The bottom line is that daycare centers should be a fun place for your dog. If your current daycare center doesn't seem to make him happy, try to come up with an alternative—especially if you are gone for long days.

Family Picnics

Everyone loves a picnic. Just picture it: the fourth of July, juicy watermelon, apple pie, yum—and then a dog comes running out of nowhere and slams into you and your plate of food. Argh! You want your dog to be a good canine citizen if you are going to take him to family and friend outings. Not only do you need to be concerned about how your dog will behave with the other dogs there, you need to be conscious of how your dog behaves with people as well. A well-trained and well-mannered dog is a joy to own. If he's good with other dogs, you can take him almost anywhere. If he's not good with other dogs, then picnics and the like may not be the best place for him to go. It's hard to manage even the best trained dog in the presence of other dogs at a place like a picnic.

You cannot simultaneously visit with people and train your dog. If you want to visit with people, leave your dog safely home or in the car with the windows cracked (weather permitting). It's impossible to carry on a conversation and train or watch your dog. If your dog is dog-friendly but unruly or under-trained, again, you may want to leave him home.

Managing Your Dog on Family Outings

An out of control dog is no fun on an outing. Keep in mind that a tired dog is much easier to manage. If you are going to a family picnic and you want to bring your dog, tire her out *beforehand*. Get her some good, hard exercise before the event.

Next, keep your dog on leash until you know the lay of the land and the rules of the area you are in. Most public picnicking places require your dog to be on leash. Respect this even if it means your dog cannot play with other dogs. If you are on private land or you are in a public area that allows dogs off leash, then you have the option of off-leash playtime.

NOTE To be considerate of the other dog owners, you should ask if other dogs are friendly before you take your

Marking Their Territory

Dogs urinate as a way to mark their territory—and as you probably already know, they do this often. This isn't a bad thing and you should allow your dog to eliminate whenever he has to.

Dogs try to lift their legs as high as possible when marking. *Credit: Sarah D. Todd*

The dog on the right is marking while showing a lowered, submissive body to the dog on the left. *Credit: Sarah D. Todd*

This dog marks while making direct eye contact with another dog. *Credit: Sarah D. Todd*

dog off leash. If your dog is friendly with other dogs, then ask the other owners if your dogs can play together.

Off-leash playtime is great fun as long as the dogs are not knocking over all the kids at the party. Sometimes dog play has to be restricted because of the exuberance that comes with doggie play-time. If the dogs are out of control, try to find an area where they can play without disturbing any-one. If that place doesn't exist, you might want to leave your dog home—if you know this ahead of time. Speaking of which, it's best if you can check out the park or area where the actual pic-nic is going to be. That way, you can find out if it is an appropriate place to bring your dog.

Picnicking with the Dog-Aggressive Dog

If your dog has issues with other dogs, try to find out what dogs will be at the family picnic. You might want to leave your dog home if there are going to be other dogs at the event. This is a sad thing for many dog owners to come to grips with—that they have to leave their dog home when their friends and family are taking their dogs out with them. You may have no choice in this matter if your dog is dog-aggressive. You must accept your dog's limitations. You cannot always have your dog-aggressive dog at family or friend events. It may be safer to leave your dog home.

If you want to try to bring your dog-aggressive dog with you to the outing, then here are some guidelines.

1. Check out who else has dogs before you take your dog out of the car.

2. See if there are any off-leash dogs in the area.

3. Muzzle train your dog in advance of the event (see section on muzzle training, page 93).

4. Keep your dog on leash and keep the peanut butter cup in her face whenever other dogs are nearby.

5. Remember, you can't focus on her and your friends at the same time. You might need to leave her in the car and bring her out for short, concentrated training sessions.

Picnics and the like can be a great place to train your dog if the other dogs are on leash and your friends are cognizant of what you are doing. If there is a chance your dog may lunge or bark at the other dogs, warn your friends before you take your dog out of the car.

Set yourself up for success by establishing your critical distance ahead of time by moving the other dogs or by taking your dog out of the car and then jogging or running to a place where your dog can be at a comfortable dis-tance. Once there, feed, feed, feed with your peanut butter cup. Keep feeding until your dog has shown she is calm and relaxed. If she does not relax, then feed for a few minutes and put her back in the car with the windows cracked (weather permitting). If she does relax, take away the peanut butter container and let her look around. If she stays controlled, you may be able to have her hang out with you on leash without feeding her. Remember: always keep the leash on if the law requires it or if you think there might be other dogs around.

Muzzling Your Dog at Family Functions

Having a muzzle on your dog in these situations can be both stressful and stress-relieving. If you can get used to the idea of your dog wearing a muzzle, it can give you a lot of freedom. As mentioned, the worst damage one dog does to another is with his teeth. If your dog is wearing a muzzle, he can still aggress, which is not great, but he can't do any damage.

The muzzle allows you to unwind some and not be so worried that your dog is going to attack another dog. It may make the difference between a dog that you can take with you and one that you have to leave at home. Only you know which your dog would prefer: to be with you and wear a muzzle, or to be at home. If you take time and train your dog to use the muzzle slowly, then most dogs will love the muzzle as much as they love the leash.

I have worked with clients who have dogs with human aggression, and the only way they could keep their dogs was to have them wear muzzles whenever they went out. One of the beautiful things about the muzzle is that other people will automatically keep their dogs away from your dog when the muzzle is on. Of course, if you are at a family or friend outing, you can probably speak with these people ahead of time so that when you show up with your muzzled dog, no one asks too many questions or gives you a hard time. Muzzles may seem controversial because they mean your dog has some type of aggression issue, but they really do give you the liberty to take your dog places you otherwise may not take them.

In all of these different outings—dog parks, doggie daycares, and picnics—remember that it's supposed to be *fun* for both you and your dog. Seize the moment and enjoy your time with your furry friend. Just do so in a safe and appropriate way depending on the circumstances.

Chapter 10  **Success Stories**

Ah, yes. Here's even *more* proof that you, too, can have a good dog. Either your dog can learn to tolerate other dogs without being aggressive, or you can modify the way you handle your dog so that he or she is easily manageable in any kind of situation where other dogs may be present.

Lisa and Jenny

In the fall of 1995, Lisa was a volunteer at the Humane Society of Chittenden County in South Burlington, Vermont. The Humane Society had recently taken in a stray litter of nine puppies with their mixed breed, floppy-eared, black and tan mom. The executive director asked Lisa if she would be interested in fostering the dog family. Lisa, who was excited about the idea of adopting a puppy, said yes and went home with the ten dogs. Well, after many weeks of caring for the dogs, Lisa had fallen in love with the mom—whom she had named Jenny. All the puppies were placed in good homes and Jenny stayed with Lisa at her home in Huntington.

As Lisa and I spoke, Jenny, now thirteen or fourteen years old, rested peacefully on a dog bed in Lisa's living room. I asked Lisa what she loved most about Jenny and she replied, "She's so relational. She's so sensitive. If I smile, she wags her tail. She's so keyed into me and has been from the very beginning. She's a cuddle-bug."

One would think Jenny was the perfect dog. However, life with her hasn't always been easy. When Lisa first adopted Jenny, she took her to regular obedience classes at The Dog School, where Jenny successfully participated in playtime with the other dogs. Even so, aggression sometimes seemed to come out of nowhere around other dogs. Lisa wasn't sure if she somehow created the problem herself or if Jenny always had issues with other dogs, but she suspected that the problem was always an underlying one and had been there all along.

Lisa said she thought she might have made the problems worse because when Jenny would react in a hostile way, Lisa would tighten up on the leash and pull Jenny in to her, as everyone does in the beginning. This tightening of the leash, as has been discussed, can cause so many problems. But Lisa didn't know what else to do, so she dragged Jenny toward her and got very nervous herself. The tight leash and Lisa's tension signaled to Jenny to be aggressive toward other dogs. Lisa said it wasn't long before everything would be fine again, but Jenny started having mixed behaviors, excitedly jumping up on her owner one minute and then lunging until she hit the end of her leash and growling like Cujo if another dog came into view. According to Lisa she had never done any damage to another dog, but she had jumped on top of them and bitten at their necks. These were definitely stressful and scary encounters.

Lisa would panic and reel Jenny in to her, and Jenny got worse. So Lisa took my Dog to Dog Communication class, the class for dog-aggressive dogs. There, Lisa learned why and how dogs become aggressive. She also learned that what was at the heart of Jenny's dog aggression was fear, and that she was never interested

in going out of her way to attack another dog. She only felt this way if she thought the other dog was threatening her, which she could feel even at thirty feet away. In her defense mode, she would try to go after the other dog.

Lisa said she learned a lot about her *own* behavior in the Dog to Dog Communication class, and learned that how she reacted to the situation made a huge difference. She said that she realized if she stayed relatively relaxed during dog to dog encounters, Jenny's response to the dogs drastically changed for the better.

Now when Lisa is out with Jenny, Lisa is hypervigilant for dogs that might set her off. When there are other dogs around, Lisa generally decides to go the other way. She tries to put herself between Jenny and the other dogs, or she chooses to walk places where there aren't other dogs around. She actively puts herself in environments where she knows there won't be any problems.

Conversely, Lisa has learned that if she shoves a hot dog in Jenny's face, she can more easily walk by other dogs. Jenny is more interested in food than she is in other dogs. Over time, Lisa has narrowed Jenny's critical distance from thirty feet to about five feet. At the five-foot distance Jenny is still willing to put her attention on the hot dog and not on the other dog. Without the food, Jenny would growl and lunge, but with the food she is able to pay attention to Lisa.

Amazingly, Lisa has done dog agility with Jenny since 1996. In agility the toughest part for Jenny is going into the competition ring. When waiting in line to go into the ring, between five and twenty dogs can be in a very close proximity with their owners. It can be a stressful environment (for both dogs and owners!). There is a lot of tension at this point in the competition because all these people are crammed together in a small space waiting for their turn to compete, and they and their dogs are incredibly anxious.

For a couple of years in the beginning, Lisa used to carry thirty-five pound Jenny into the ring because it was easiest for both of them. She said it was very funny that Jenny would growl and give the hairy eyeball to all of the other dogs, but she would laugh because she knew her dog couldn't do anything. Once in the ring, and after much training, Jenny would stay focused on her task and not leave the ring or show any interest in the other dogs. Jenny would perform the agility obstacles and competed well, achieving many titles.

I wondered how Lisa had been able to maintain such fantastic control over Jenny, since no food is allowed in the agility ring. At agility trials there can be hundreds of people and dogs in a confined space. Usually competitors put up shade tents and crate their dogs under these tents. There are dogs *everywhere*. Lisa often puts her tent far away from the other dogs so that Jenny doesn't have to feel pressured or stressed out by other canines. Jenny is able to relax this way. Lisa scopes out places to walk and loosen her up that are far from the other

dogs. When she does have to get close to the other dogs, to get her in the ring, Lisa doesn't carry Jenny anymore. Jenny can now walk right by other dogs as long as food is in her face. Through massive desensitization training and the Dog to Dog Communication class, Lisa has taught Jenny to stay calm in the presence of other dogs.

I asked Lisa if she felt going to agility trials and being around all the other dogs had a negative impact on Jenny. Her response was that she thinks it *can* have a negative impact in that it can be exhausting for Jenny to be around dogs all day, but that's why Lisa won't locate her tent where other dogs will pass it. But in terms of actually being in the ring, she doesn't think Jenny is bothered at all.

Today, Jenny's training has advanced so far that she was even able to compete in an event called "Pairs," in which dog caretakers pass a baton from one person to another who is waiting in the ring with a dog. The dogs have to come within a few feet of each other while the owners are running. Lisa says she was able to do this because she could keep Jenny focused on her by talking to her and asking her to sit or down before she handed off the baton. She realized that Jenny is basically scared of other dogs. If Lisa gave Jenny an excuse to pay attention to her, she would take it.

Now retired, Jenny no longer competes in agility. She lounges around the house with her two canine companions, Fly and Spicey, both mixed breed pound dogs. Lisa says Jenny "rules the roost" and has to "put Fly in his place" occasionally, but she is mostly a gentle boss. If Lisa throws a tennis ball, Jenny tells Fly it's hers but doesn't go after him. These days she has decent enough dog communication skills and is able to get along fine with her housemates. She actually plays with Fly a lot and lets Spicey sleep on one side of the bed next to her owner.

Lisa says that she and Jenny are soul mates and that her dog has taught her so much. Through intense and dedicated training, Lisa and Jenny have been able to succeed at much in life.

Gregg and Trout

Trout stretches out on a rug by the door, her six doggie brothers and sisters lying in various locations in the combined kitchen/dining room area of her house. Gregg got six-month-old Trout in 1998 from a shelter in Palmer, Alaska, while traveling around the state on an extended vacation. Her heritage unknown, Gregg calls the female dog a Norwegian Elkhound/Alaskan Malamute mix. She is a beautiful dog with long gray, silver, and black hair covering her sixty-five pound body.

Gregg begins by telling me that what he loves the most about Trout is her affection for Ted, Gregg's ten-year-old male Bernese Mountain dog. Trout and Ted fell in love at first sight and to this day, Trout follows Ted around the house and on hikes. Basically, anywhere Ted goes, Trout wants to be.

"I love her personality," Gregg says. "She's a bit shy with people and sits back and waits for attention and then will come over. She comes to me when I am in a bad mood and she sits by me." Gregg also said Trout is a wonderful hiking and backpacking companion. Their relationship started with camping trips in the Alaskan wilderness and now continues in the hills of Vermont where they live together with six other dogs, two cats, two turtles, one tank full of fish, and Gregg's wife, Samantha.

But, as was the case with Jenny, looks can be deceiving. Gregg said that when he returned to Vermont from Alaska, he used to take Trout and Ted to the local dog park (where he met Samantha by the way!). Initially, Trout was fine with all the other dogs. Mostly scared of them, she never fought or had issues. As she matured, however, things began to change. According to Gregg, Trout started with posturing at other dogs—standing tall and forward and just acting pushy. On hikes, Trout would initially give a high-pitched whine but then would run up the trail and literally go after other dogs, intimidating them with her size and behavior. On one visit to Samantha's parent's house, Trout ran down a path and *really* scared a woman with a five-month-old Golden Retriever puppy. On another occasion, a friend of Gregg's came to visit with her dog and when the friend opened the door, Trout ran out and immediately went after the new dog. Trout has never punctured or injured another dog but her behavior was rude and inappropriate. Hiking and camping became no fun for the pair, and Gregg knew he desperately needed help. He sought out my services at The Dog School.

Gregg enrolled Trout in my Dog to Dog Communication course. There he learned that Trout mostly had mild dominance aggression. It was considered mild because while she came on strong, she never really *intended* to hurt another dog. Gregg says she would "come out of the gate" with her hackles up—very tall and domineering—but then she would quickly turn away after her initial "attack." She definitely had issues, but Gregg learned they were probably manageable with training.

In the later weeks of the communication class we worked extensively on the exercises look, sit, heel, and come. Gregg began to teach these things to Trout. Trout seemed to enjoy their training sessions and she took to it all pretty quickly. "I was able to get a really reliable recall over the course of several months," Gregg says. "Now when I hike with Trout, I am able to call her back if I see another dog. She comes to me and sits and waits at my side while the other dog passes. I find if I put the leash on and have a container of peanut butter or other high-quality treats, Trout will pay attention to me and not the other dog." Gregg was happily able to resume hiking with Trout and taking her places to which he had stopped going. He said that camping several times a year has become a real joy for them again.

But then there was a huge change in Trout's life. Samantha started a dog rescue organization called Random Rescue based out of their house in Williamstown, Vermont. In Samantha's rescue, the ownerless dogs are all fostered in the house and live with Gregg and Samantha's dogs as part of their pack. This posed a real challenge for Trout.

Without any intervention, Trout starts by making a high-pitched whine when she first sees a new dog. Then she sniffs. She usually will show a moment's hesitation, which is followed by a deep, throaty growl. That's when everyone gets pulled apart. She also triggers on movement. If a rescue dog runs in the house, Trout will go after him and either Gregg or Samantha has to pull her away. Caution has to be used with Trout at all times.

After attempting various methods, the couple finally found a way to introduce Trout to the rescue dogs with little problem. First they lock up all their dogs. Next, they bring them into the same room as the new rescue dog, slowly and one at a time. Trout is always the last to come into the room. If they hold her by the collar and bring her to greet the new dog this way, they found that she will typically stay relaxed. They still have to watch her if the rescue dog runs through the house, but other than that she is fine as long as there is a controlled introduction. This is not a method that often works for dogs, but it has worked well for Trout.

Not only was Trout dog-aggressive, she also had personal space issues. As we chatted, Toby, an older male Cocker Spaniel that Gregg rescued many years ago, approached Trout. She barely lifted her head and let out a low growl. Until this time, Trout had lain silently on her rug, occasionally switching from side to side but not moving beyond that. "If she's lying on her mat and resting she will go after other dogs," Gregg warned. He said she does it because she's sleeping.

I wondered if she had specific beds she guarded, but both Gregg and Samantha said she would guard any bed that she was sleeping on. They said that in the car she'll be lounging all stretched out and all the other dogs will be huddled in a corner, cramped and staying away from her. Gregg crates Trout now when she's in the car because he's afraid a fight could break out when she growls at another dog. The crate has been a wonderful management tool to make car rides safe.

Other than guarding her space, Trout does fine with her own pack these days. She enjoys outings with them—especially camping trips with Gregg. When necessary, Gregg and Samantha continue to crate Trout but her problems have definitely subsided.

Liz, John, and Dover

Deemed too big for his original home, ninety-five-pound purebred black Labrador retriever, Dover, ended up at Labrador Retriever Rescue, Inc., based in Hamilton, Massachusetts, when he was only a year old. Shortly afterward, in May 2005, he was adopted by Liz and John, who had been looking for a Lab to join their family.

"We said we'd take almost any dog but didn't want to have a dog with separation anxiety," John recalls. "Of course, we ended up with a dog with a severe case of it." And that's what originally brought the couple to The Dog School.

The last straw was when Liz and John went home to find Dover had broken out of his third crate. It looked as if a tornado had blown threw their home. It was obvious that Dover was very distressed. "I couldn't believe how much damage he was able to do in one day," Liz said. In addition, it was obvious that Dover had been excessively drooling and going to the bathroom in the crate before breaking out of it. He definitely had separation anxiety, and wasn't crate trained like the Lab rescue organization had said he was.

Dover had also started being unfriendly toward dogs he came in contact with on the street. On more than one occasion he would pull on his leash to get to other dogs, and he didn't seem to have a friendly encounter on his mind. Although Liz was used to handling horses, she wasn't quite sure how to deal with Dover and his eager attempts to dart after other dogs. She would begin to panic and didn't know what to do about the situation.

Everyone from friends to vets to pet store associates seemed to have an opinion on how to handle the rambunctious pup, but nothing seemed to work. After the third or fourth incident of dragging Liz on the leash, Dover pulled her so abruptly that she hurt her knee. That's when she learned about The Dog School.

The couple came in for a consult and described how Dover "literally lunged and dragged you over when he saw another dog." Dover had the classic aggressive dog body language: a high, flagging tail, hackles up at the withers, growling, and barking deeply. John mentioned that if Dover ever managed to get to the dog he was going after, he would attempt to pummel it. He noted that as aggressive as he seemed, he would never actually puncture another dog—except for once.

One day, a friend's twelve-year-old Coonhound mix bit Dover and left a puncture wound on his nose. The next time they encountered each other on a hiking excursion, Dover went after the Coonhound mix and they both bit each other. "It's the only time he's bit another dog," says Liz. But it was enough to cause concern for her and her husband.

Living in small city, Liz and John often encountered other dogs on their daily outings. Being exercise fanatics, they had hoped that Dover could accompany them on jogs and hikes throughout New England. The first summer they had Dover, John was training for a triathlon and Liz tried to bring Dover to his training sessions because his separation anxiety made it really hard to leave him home alone. However, if there was another dog in the crowd, even if they were in a big field, he tried to lunge toward it. This posed a huge problem for the active couple.

Before they came to The Dog School they had tried everything, according to John. He said they had tried the choke chain and prong collar. Someone at a local pet supply store suggested trying the "alpha roll"—literally pinning Dover to the ground. "We tried it even though it made us cry," John admitted. "We were just desperate and willing to try anything." But even that didn't work. The minute Dover was able to get up, he attempted to lunge at the other dog all over again.

They met with Sam, the executive director at The Dog School, and wanted to tackle the separation anxiety and crating issues first and foremost. Sam talked about all kinds of options for the separation anxiety, and eventually John and Liz learned how to gradually reintroduce Dover to the crate. Once Dover got that down, they continued to crate him until his spastic behavior began to stop. One day, a friend with a dog moved in with the couple for a few months. When left alone together, the dogs were completely fine. It seemed that Dover just waited by the door. He lived with the other dog, a Husky, for two or three months and then when the Husky and his owner moved out, it was decided that Dover's separation anxiety was cured.

Next on the agenda was addressing Dover's dog to dog aggression. Liz openly says that this was a bigger issue for her. "I felt so bad because he's such a good dog and I was embarrassed to take him in public because he was so unruly with other dogs. People hated him and made rude comments about him."

The executive director evaluated Dover with her other dogs. It looked to her as though

Dover may have been tied out in his life with his previous owner, and spent a great deal of time lunging and pulling toward other dogs. "So we did the thing with the peanut butter cup," says Liz, referring to the desensitization training. "And we used the concentrated breath spray," adds John. "It was like the good cop/bad cop with the peanut butter and breath spray."

Sam also taught the couple how to properly use the head halter—which proved to be impressive. Once wearing it, Dover seemed to turn into a completely different dog. Liz said that they practiced these newly learned techniques almost religiously. "The peanut butter, breath spray, and halter . . . We first tried it at The Dog School. Then we started going to parking lots. We tag-teamed him. One of us would have the treats and one of us would have the spray. It worked really, really well. It took a long time but we kept going."

But Dover had a relapse one day. Fortunately, that slip-up was at the beginning of the training and the two dogs were just too close together for Dover's comfort. His critical distance was being invaded and he instinctively aggressed. Liz tried to explain to the other dogs' owners on the bike path that her dog needed space, but as it often happens, the other dog owners didn't have control of their dogs at the time. Liz was with her sister, and the training tools didn't work. Liz broke down and lost it as she couldn't control her poorly behaving dog. "It was ugly," John admits. "But we just kept at it."

John and Liz did the parking lot training for a few months and then signed up Dover for a basic beginner obedience class. John planned to use a spray bottle with water, but eventually the dog would only act up for the first five minutes of class. Using the water bottle seemed to work wonders, and eventually Dover became really good at playtime. "We thought we would have to take him to the Dog to Dog Communication class, but actually he was great," says Liz.

Later, after intermediate and advanced obedience training, the couple decided to take agility classes with Dover. He hardly even needed to use his head halter anymore. "We put it on him when we first got there and then we could take it off and he was fine," Liz said. Sometimes there would be a dog he didn't like, especially if that dog had issues with other dogs, but he could go to agility class and do the obstacles off leash and behave himself along with the other dogs just fine.

One would never believe that today Dover is an active therapy dog! With therapy dog work, you often have to work closely with other dogs. "He's fine with dogs he's known for a long time," says John. His hair will still sometimes stand up for about two seconds when he first sees another dog, but then he will be fine, they say. "Sometimes the other dogs are all over him and he's okay," says John. "And the kids," he adds, "the kids are all over him, too, and he's great." Dover makes weekly visits to the local library as a member of Therapy Dogs of Vermont. "He loves going," says Liz. "We try to educate the kids that they should ask to pet him first, but they just run up to him and hug him and Dover loves it."

Sandy and Django

Even after twelve days of boarding, ninety-pound, two-year-old, Django still paces and bounces around the room. "We don't know what to call him," his caretaker Sandy says regarding his breed. Django is a large, blue merle dog with long, silky hair and crimped fluff behind his ears.

While Django obviously has a zest for life and is incredibly fun to be around, he's not the type of dog a first-time dog owner would probably want because of his high energy level. He has a hard time sitting still and constantly climbs in and out of people's laps and dances all over the room.

Django, a stray, was adopted by Sandy and her family after their Border Collie had died at the age of fifteen. The family was going to wait a while to get a new dog, but Sandy couldn't stop herself from perusing the rescue sites on the Internet. "I talked to my husband and said 'Why are we waiting?' Then Steve got online and came home and said, 'Look . . .' and there was a picture of Django." Within three days Django had been adopted by the Morris family.

His liveliness and sense of humor are some of what Sandy loves the most about Django, but when asked what has been hard about living with him she smiles and responds, "His exuberance." The Morrises live in a suburban neighborhood, and Django pulls hard to try to get to the other dogs in the area whenever they're out for walks.

Even though Django has a large fenced-in yard, Sandy enjoys daily outings around the vicinity of her house, too. She said that she can take him off leash in the woods behind her house, but she always has to keep him on leash around the neighborhood. He's very attracted to other dogs and makes every effort to go say hello. And that's the hard part. He gets way too excited around other dogs. Out in the woods, when he and Sandy meet up with other dogs, it's perfectly fine, says Sandy. But in the woods, Django has the ability to run over to the other dogs because the other dogs are off leash too. "People who walk their dogs in these woods all have their dogs off leash," Sandy explains. "We've never had a bad encounter in the woods."

She says that Django is much better behaved off leash than on. When he's on leash, problems arise. His need to say hello all the time gets him into trouble with other dogs. "That's that exuberant part I was talking about. It's the leash thing," Sandy explains. "He's not aggressive; he's just jumping up and down and tugging on the leash to go see the other dog."

He used to drag Sandy down the sidewalk when she took him on leashed outings. But with some training advice from The Dog School, Sandy has taught Django to come back to her and sit at her side. "We have all these little dogs on our street. Westies, toy miniature Schnauzers, Chihuahuas—we've got everything," says Sandy. "Django just wants them all. When

I run with him [as opposed to walking] he's more focused and I can keep him with me really well. But when we're walking I have to stop and call him back to me," says Sandy. Then she can ask the other dog owner if the dogs can meet.

Always on leash in the neighborhood and with dog turkey jerky in her pocket, Sandy has learned to maintain control of Django at all times. She stops and inquires if the other dog is friendly and then if so, Django is allowed to have a short, leashed interaction with the other dog. If the new dog is not friendly, then Sandy walks on by with Django at her side.

While Django's high energy level is obvious, there are ways manage him so that he doesn't go berserk every time he comes in contact with another dog. "That's why I run him in the woods every day," says Sandy. "Like today, we met up with a Golden Retriever and they played for about fifteen minutes." Eventually the Golden Retriever's owner tried unsuccessfully to get her dog back as the two pups romped around. "Django was great," said Sandy. "He helped me get her dog back to her." More importantly, he went to her when she called him.

I looked down at the hyper but well-trained pup in front of me. "Good job," I cooed to Django and smiled to myself. Another poster child for dog adoption.

Resources

Groups and Organizations

Association of Pet Dog Trainers
150 Executive Ctr. Dr. Box 35
Greenville, SC 29615
Phone: (800) PET-DOGS
E-mail: information@apdt.com
Web site: www.apdt.com
Referrals to dog trainers nationwide. Mostly positive reinforcement trainers.

The Dog School
55 Leroy Rd.
Williston, VT 05495
Phone: (802) 860-1111
E-mail: info@thedogschool.biz
Web site: www.thedogschool.biz
Jamie Shaw's dog training school.

Dogwise. All Things Dog.
Phone: (800) 776-2665
Web site: www.dogwise.com
Huge library of dog books and dog products.

Random Rescue
140 Casino Road
Williamstown, VT 05679
Phone: (802) 433-5912
E-mail: randomrescue@gmail.com
Web site: www.randomrescue.org
Places adoptable dogs into loving homes.

The Whole Dog Journal
P.O. Box 420235
Palm Coast, FL 32142
Phone: (800) 829-9165
Web site: www.whole-dog-journal.com
Periodical that specializes in "effective holistic health-care methods and successful nonviolent training."

Books

Aloff, Brenda. *Canine Body Language: A Photographic Guide Interpreting the Native Language of the Domestic Dog.* Wenatchee, WA: Dogwise Publishing, 2005.

Clothier, Suzanne. *Bones Would Rain From the Sky.* New York: Warner Books, 2002.

Coppinger, Raymond and Lorna Coppinger. *Dogs: A New Understanding of Canine Origin, Behavior and Evolution.* Chicago, IL: University of Chicago Press, 2001.

Donaldson, Jean. *The Culture Clash.* Berkley, CA: James & Kenneth Publishers, 1996.

Fogle, Bruce, DVM, MRCVS. *The Dog's Mind: Understanding Your Dog's Behavior.* New York: Howell Book House, 1990.

Grandin, Temple and Catherine Johnson. *Animals in Translation.* Orlando, FL: Harcourt Books, 2005.

McConnell, Patricia B., PhD. *The Other End of the Leash.* New York: Ballantine Books, 2002.

McConnell, Patricia B., PhD, and Karen B. London, PhD. *Feisty Fido.* Black Earth, WI: Dog's Best Friend, Ltd., 2003.

Miller, Pat. *The Power of Positive Dog Training.* New York: Wiley Publishing, Inc., 2001.

Pryor, Karen. *Don't Shoot the Dog! The New Art of Teaching and Training.* New York: Bantam Books, 1999.

Scott, John Paul and John L. Fuller. *Genetics and the Social Behavior of the Dog.* Chicago, IL: University of Chicago Press, 1965.

Sternberg, Sue. *Successful Dog Adoption.* Indianapolis, IN: Wiley Publishing, Inc., 2003.

Index

About the Author

Jamie Shaw founded The Dog School in 1987 when she saw a need for a new kind of dog training. The school uses the theory of animal learning to train and teach dogs to be very user-friendly for their owners. Shaw teaches dog to dog communication, agility, and obedience classes and also offers behavioral consultations. She lives with her husband, daughter, five dogs, four cats, one lizard, one fish, and four rescued pot-bellied pigs (in the barn, of course) in Huntington, Vermont.